# ELITES AND
# SOCIETY

# ELITES
# AND
# SOCIETY

T. B. BOTTOMORE

BASIC BOOKS, INC.
*Publishers*
NEW YORK

*First published by C. A. Watts & Co. Ltd., London, in*
*"The New Thinker's Library," General Editor: Raymond Williams*

# CONTENTS

v

# THE ELITE: CONCEPT AND IDEOLOGY

THE word "*élite*" was used in the seventeenth century to describe commodities of particular excellence; and the usage was later extended to refer to superior social groups, such as crack military units or the higher ranks of the nobility.[1] In the English language the earliest known use of "elite," according to the *Oxford English Dictionary*, is in 1823, at which time it was already applied to social groups. But the term did not become widely used in social and political writing until late in the nineteenth century in Europe, or until the 1930s in Britain and America, when it was diffused through the sociological theories of elites, notably in the writings of Vilfredo Pareto.

Pareto defined "elite" in two different ways. He began with a very general definition: "Let us assume that in every branch of human activity each individual is given an index which stands as a sign of his capacity, very much the way grades are given in the various subjects in examinations in school. The highest type of lawyer, for instance, will be given 10. The man who does not get a client will be given 1—reserving zero for the man who is an out-and-out idiot. To the man who has made his millions—honestly or dishonestly as the case may be—we will give 10. To the man who has earned his thousands we will give 6; to such as just manage to keep out of the poor-house 1, keeping zero for those who get in . . . And so on for all the branches of human activity ... So let us make a class of the people who have the highest indices in their branch of activity, and to that class give the name of *elite*."[2] Pareto himself does not make any further use of this concept of elite; it serves merely to emphasize the inequality of individual endowment in every sphere of social life, and as the starting point for a definition of the "governing elite," which is his real subject matter. "For the particular investigation with which we are engaged, a study of the social equilibrium, it will help if we further divide that class [the elite] into two classes: a *governing elite*, comprising individuals who directly or indirectly play some considerable part in government, and a *non-governing elite*, comprising the rest ... So we get two strata in a population: (1) A lower stratum, the *non-elite*, with whose possible influence on government we are not just here concerned; then (2) a higher stratum, *the elite*, which is divided into two: (*a*) a governing *elite*; (*b*) a non-governing *elite*."[3]

It is not difficult to discover, from Pareto's earlier writings, how he arrived at this conception. In his *Cours d'économie politique*[4] he had propounded the idea of a normal curve of the distribution of wealth in a society. In *Les systèmes social-istes*[5] he went on to argue, first, that if individuals were arranged according to other criteria, such as their level of intelligence, aptitude for mathematics, musical talent, moral character, etc., there would probably result distribution curves similar to that for wealth; and secondly, that if individuals were arranged according to their degree of political and social power or influence, it would be found in most societies that the same individuals occupied the same place in this hierarchy as in the hierarchy of wealth. "The so-called upper classes are also usually the richest. *These classes represent an elite, an 'aristocracy'.* ..."[6]

Nevertheless, there is an important difference in the for-mulation of the question in *The Mind and Society*, for Pareto here concerns himself not with a curve of distribution of certain attributes (including power and influence), but with a simple opposition between those who have power, the "governing elite," and those who have none, the masses. This change in Pareto's conception may well have owed something to the work of Gaetano Mosca, who was the first to make a systematic distinction between "elite" and masses —though using other terms—and to attempt the construction of a new science of politics on this foundation.[7] Mosca expressed his fundamental idea in these words: "Among the constant facts and tendencies that are to be found in all political organisms, one is so obvious that it is apparent to the most casual eye. In all societies—from societies that are very meagrely developed and have barely attained the dawnings of civilization, down to the most advanced and powerful societies—two classes of people appear—a class that rules and a class that is ruled. The first class, always the less numerous, performs all political functions, monopolizes power and enjoys the advantages that power brings, whereas the second, the more numerous class, is directed and controlled by the first, in a manner that is now more or less legal, now more or less arbitrary and violent . . ."[8] Mosca explains the rule of the minority over the majority by the fact that the former is organized ". . . the dominion of an organized minority, obeying a single impulse, over the unorganized majority is inevitable. The power of any minority is irresistible as against each single individual in the majority, who stands alone before the totality of the organized minority. At the same time, the minority is organized for the very reason that it is a minority"—and also by the fact that the minority is usually composed of superior individuals—". . . members of a ruling minority regularly have some attribute, real or apparent, which is highly esteemed and very influential in the society in which they live."[9]

Both Mosca and Pareto, therefore, were concerned with elites in the sense of groups of people who either exercised directly, or were in a position to influence very strongly the exercise of, political power. At the same time, they recognized that the "governing elite" or "political class" is itself composed of distinct social groups. Pareto observed that the "upper stratum of society, the *elite*, nominally contains certain groups of people, not always very sharply defined, that are called aristocracies," and he went on to refer to "military, religious, and commercial aristocracies and plutocracies."[10] The point was made more sharply in a study of elites in France by a pupil of Pareto, Marie Kolabinska, who discussed explicitly the movement of individuals between the different sub-groups of the governing elite, and set out to examine in some detail the history of four such groups: the rich, the nobles, the armed aristocracy and the clergy.[11] Nevertheless, Pareto is always inclined to emphasize more strongly the division between *the* governing elite and the non-elite, and it is Mosca who examines more thoroughly the composition of the elite itself, especially in the modern democratic societies. Thus he refers to "the various party organizations into which the political class is divided," and which have to compete for the votes of the more numerous classes; and later on he remarks that "it cannot be denied that the representative system [of government] provides a way for many different social forces to participate in the political system and, therefore, to balance and limit the influence of other social forces and the influence of bureaucracy in particular." This last passage also reveals a considerable divergence between Pareto and Mosca in their interpretation of the development of political systems. Pareto always emphasizes the universality of the distinction between governing elite and masses, and he reserves his most scathing comments for the modern notions of "democracy," "humanitarianism" and "progress." Mosca, on the other hand, is prepared to recognize, and in a qualified way to approve, the distinctive features of modern democracy; in his first book, it is true, he observes that in a parliamentary democracy, "the representative is not elected by the voters but, as a rule, has himself elected by them ... or ... his friends have him elected"; but in his later works he concedes that the majority may, through its representatives, have a certain control over government policy. As Meisel notes, it is only in his criticism of Marx that Mosca makes a sharp disjunction between masses and minorities; for the most part he presents a more subtle and complex theory in which the political class itself is influenced and restrained by a variety of "social forces" (representing numerous different interests in society), and also by the moral unity of the society as a whole which is expressed in the rule of law. In Mosca's theory, an elite does not simply rule by force and fraud, but "represents," in some sense, the interests and purposes of important and influential groups in the society.

There is another element, too, in Mosca's theory which modifies its original stark outlines. In modern times, the elite is not simply raised high above the rest of society; it is intimately connected with society through a sub-elite, a much larger group which comprises, to all intents and purposes, the whole "new middle class" of civil servants, managers and white collar workers, scientists and engineers, scholars and intellectuals. This group does not only supply recruits to the elite (the ruling class in the narrow sense); it is itself a vital element in the government of society, and Mosca observes that "the stability of any political organism depends on the level of morality, intelligence and activity that this second stratum has attained." It is not unreasonable, then, to claim, as did Gramsci, that Mosca's "political class ... is a puzzle. One does not exactly understand what Mosca means, so fluctuating and elastic is the notion. Sometimes he seems to think of the middle class, sometimes of men of property in general, and then again of those who call themselves 'the educated.' But on other occasions Mosca apparently has in mind the 'political personnel.' "[12] And later, with more certainty: "Mosca's 'political class' is nothing but the intellectual section of the ruling group. Mosca's term approximates Pareto's *elite* concept—another attempt to interpret the historical phenomenon of the intelligentsia and its function in political and social life."[13]

The conceptual scheme which Mosca and Pareto have handed down thus comprises the following common notions: in every society there is, and must be, a minority which rules over the rest of society; this minority—the "political class" or "governing elite," composed of those who occupy the posts of political command and, more vaguely, those who can directly influence political decisions—undergoes changes in its membership over a period of time, ordinarily by the recruitment of new individual members from the lower strata of society, sometimes by the incorporation of new social groups, and occasionally by the complete replacement of the established elite by a "counter-elite," as occurs in revolutions. This phenomenon, the "circulation of elites," will be examined more fully in a later chapter. From this point, the conceptions of Pareto and Mosca diverge. Pareto insists more strongly upon the separation between rulers and ruled in every society, and dismisses the view that a democratic political system differs from any other in this respect.[14] He explains the circulation of elites in mainly psychological terms, making use of the idea of residues (sentiments) which he has set out at great length in the earlier parts of *The Mind and Society*. Mosca, on the other hand, is much more aware of the heterogeneity of the elite, the higher stratum of the political class, itself; of the interests or social forces which are represented in it; and, in the case of modern societies, of its intimate bonds with the rest of society, principally through the lower stratum of the political class, the "new middle class." Thus Mosca also allows that there is a difference between modern democracies and other types of polity, and to some extent he recognizes that there is interaction between the ruling minority and the majority, instead of a simple dominance by the former over the latter. Finally, Mosca explains the circulation of elites sociologically as well as psychologically, in so far as he accounts for the rise of new elites (or of new elements in the elite) in part by the emergence of social forces which represent new interests (e.g. technological or economic interests) in the society.[15]

Later studies of elites have followed Pareto and Mosca, especially the latter, closely in their concern with problems of political power. Thus H. D. Lasswell, both in his early writings which were commended by Mosca himself, and more recently in the Hoover Institute Studies on elites, has devoted himself particularly to the study of the political elite, which he defines in the following terms: "The political elite comprises the power holders of a body politic. The power holders include the leadership and the social formations from which leaders typically come, and to which accountability is maintained, during a given period."[16] The difference from the conceptions of Pareto and Mosca is that the *political elite* is here distinguished from other elites which are less closely associated with the exercise of power, although they may have a considerable social influence, and that the idea of "social formations" (including social classes) from which elites are typically recruited is reintroduced into a scheme of thought from which, especially in Pareto's theory, it had been expelled. As we shall see in a moment, the idea of elites was originally conceived in opposition to the idea of social classes. A similar development is apparent in the writings of Raymond Aron, who has also been chiefly concerned with the elite in the sense of a governing minority, but has attempted to establish a relation between the elite and social classes,[17] has insisted upon the plurality of elites in modern societies, and has examined the social influence of the intellectual elite, which does not ordinarily form part of the system of political power.[18]

The fresh distinctions and refinements which have been made in the concept of the elite call for a more discriminating terminology than has been employed hitherto.[19] The term "elite(s)" is now generally applied, in fact, to functional, mainly occupational, groups which have high status (for whatever reason) in a society; and henceforward I shall use it, without qualification, in this sense. The study of such elites is fruitful in several ways: the size of the elites, the number of different elites, their relations with each other and with the groups that wield political power, are among the most important facts which have to be considered in distinguishing between different types of society and in accounting for changes in social structure; so, too, is the closed or open character of the elites, or in other words, the nature of the recruitment of their members and the degree of social mobility which this implies. If the general term "elite" is to be applied to these functional groups, we shall need another term for the minority which rules a society, which is not a functional group in exactly the same sense, and which is in any case of such great social importance that it deserves to be given a distinctive name. I shall use here Mosca's term, the "political class," to refer to all those groups which exercise political power or influence, and are directly engaged in struggles for political leadership; and I shall distinguish within the political class a smaller group, the political elite, which comprises those individuals who actually exercise political power in a society at any given time. The extent of the political elite is, therefore, relatively easy to determine: it will include members of the government and of the high administration, military leaders, and, in some cases, politically influential families of an aristocracy or royal house and leaders of powerful economic enterprises. It is less easy to set the boundaries of the political class; it will, of course, include the political elite, but it may also include "counter-elites" comprising the leaders of political parties which are out of office, and representatives of new social interests or classes (e.g. trade union leaders), as well as groups of businessmen, and intellectuals who are active in politics. The political class, therefore, is composed of a number of groups which may be engaged in varying degrees of co-operation, competition or conflict with each other.

The concept of the political elite was presented by Mosca and Pareto as a key term in a new social science,[20] but it had another aspect which is scarcely less apparent in their writings; namely, that it formed part of a political doctrine which was opposed to, or critical of, modern democracy, and still more opposed to modern socialism.[21] C. J. Friedrich has drawn attention to the fact that the nineteenth-century European doctrines of rule by an elite of superior individuals—doctrines which encompassed Carlyle's philosophy of the hero and Nietzsche's vision of the superman as well as the more prosaic studies of Mosca, Pareto and Burckhardt—were "all off-spring of a society containing as yet many feudal remnants," and that these doctrines represented so many different attempts to revive ancient ideas of social hierarchy and to erect ob-stacles to the spread of democratic notions.[22] The social environment of such doctrines is defined still more narrowly by G. Lukács, who suggests that the problem of political leadership was raised by sociologists precisely in those countries which had not succeeded in establishing a genuine bourgeois democracy (i.e. in which the feudal elements were especially strong); and he points to Max Weber's concept of "charisma" (in Germany) and Pareto's concept of "elites" (in Italy) as similar and typical manifestations of this preoccupation.[23]

The opposition between the idea of elites and the idea of democracy may be expressed in two forms: first, that the insistence in the elite theories upon the inequality of individual endowment runs counter to a fundamental strand in democratic political thought, which is inclined rather to emphasize an underlying equality of individuals; and secondly, that the notion of a governing minority contradicts the democratic theory of majority rule. But this opposition need not be by any means so rigorous and extreme as appears at first sight. If democracy is regarded as being primarily a political system, it may well be argued, as many have done, that "government *by* the people" (i.e. the effective rule of the majority) is impossible in practice, and that the significance of political democracy is primarily that the positions of power in society are open in principle to everyone, that there is competition for power, and that the holders of power at any time are accountable to the electorate. Schumpeter presented such a view of democracy, which has since been widely accepted, when he defined the democratic method as "that institutional arrangement for arriving at political decisions in which individuals acquire the power to decide by means of a competitive struggle for the people's vote."[24] Similarly, Karl Mannheim, who at an earlier stage had seen in the views of the elite theorists an irrational justification of "direct action," and of unconditional subordination to a leader,[25] came later to regard such theories as being compatible with democracy: "... the actual shaping of policy is in the hands of elites; but this does not mean to say that the society is not democratic. For it is sufficient for democracy that the individual citizens, though prevented from taking a direct part in government all the time, have at least the *possibility* of making their aspirations felt at certain intervals."[26]

Moreover, it can equally well be argued that, even if democracy is regarded as comprising more than a political system, it is still compatible with elite theories; for the idea of equality which democracy as a form of society may be held to imply can easily be re-interpreted as "equality of opportunity." Democracy will then be treated as a type of society in which the elites—economic and cultural, as well as political—are "open" in principle, and are in fact recruited from different social strata on the basis of individual merit. This conception of the place of elites in a democracy is actually suggested by the theory of the circulation of elites, and it is stated explicitly in Mosca's writings.

It needs to be emphasized at this point that both the conceptions I have discussed—that of political competition, and that of equality of opportunity—can be presented as corollaries of liberal, or *laissez-faire*, economic theory. Schumpeter was quite aware of this: "This concept (of competition for political leadership) presents similar difficulties as the concept of competition in the economic sphere, with which it may be usefully compared;"[27] and a more recent writer has stated the connection still more forcefully: ". . . the theory of elites  is, essentially, only a refinement of social *laissez-faire*. The doctrine of opportunity in education is a mere silhouette of the doctrine of economic individualism, with its emphasis on competition and 'getting-on.' "[28] In one sense, therefore, the elite theories of Pareto and Mosca were not (and those of their successors are not now) opposed to the general idea of democracy. Their original and main antagonist was, in fact, socialism, and especially Marxist socialism. As Mosca wrote:

"In the world in which we are living socialism will be arrested only if a realistic political science succeeds in demolishing the metaphysical and optimistic methods that prevail at present in social studies . . ." This "realistic science," which Pareto, Weber, Michels and others in different ways helped to further, was intended above all to refute Marx's theory of social classes on two essential points: first, to show that the Marxist conception of a "ruling *class*" is erroneous, by demonstrating the continual circulation of elites, which prevents in most societies, and especially in modern industrial societies, the formation of a stable and closed ruling class; and secondly, to show that a classless society is impossible, since in every society there is, and must be, a minority which actually rules. As Meisel so aptly comments: " 'Elite' was originally a middle class notion . . . (In the Marxist theory) . . . the proletariat is to be the ultimate class which will usher in the classless society. Not so. Rather, the history of all societies, past and future, is the history of its ruling classes . . . there will always be a ruling class, and therefore exploitation. This is the anti-socialist, specifically anti-Marxist, bent of the elitist theory as it unfolds in the last decade of the nineteenth century."[29] The elitist theories also oppose socialist doctrines in a more general way, by substituting for the notion of a class which rules by virtue of economic or military power, the notion of an elite which rules because of the superior qualities of its members. As Kolabinska says, " . . . the principal notion conveyed by the term 'elite' is that of superiority . . ."[30]

These reflections upon the ideological elements in elite theories provoke some further questions. It is possible, as I have suggested, to reconcile the idea of elites with democratic social theories; yet the early exponents of elite theories were undoubtedly hostile to democracy (although Mosca changed his views somewhat after his experience of Fascist rule in

Italy, and became a cautious defender of some aspects of democratic government), and the hostility is still more marked in the case of those, such as Carlyle and Nietzsche, who presented social myths rather than scientific theories of politics. How is this to be explained? There is, first, the fact that these nineteenth-century thinkers conceived democracy in a different way, as a stage in the "revolt of the masses" leading with apparent necessity towards socialism. In criticizing democracy, therefore, they were, in an indirect way, combating socialism itself. It should be noticed, further, that the elite theorists themselves have had an important influence in producing the new definitions of democracy, such as that of Schumpeter, which are then held up as being compatible with the notion of elites. These developments in social thought, which have affected our modern conceptions of both democracy and socialism, will be examined more closely in a later chapter.

Another characteristic of the elite theories has been reproduced in many recent social theories which are directed against socialism; it is that, while these theories criticize the determinism which they find especially in Marxism, they themselves tend to establish an equally strict kind of determinism. The fundamental argument of the elite theorists is not merely that every known society has been divided into two strata—a ruling minority and a majority which is ruled —but that all societies *must* be so divided. In what respect is this less deterministic than Marxism? For whether men are obliged to attain the classless society or are necessarily prevented from ever attaining it, are they not equally unfree? It may be objected that the cases are not alike: that the elite theorists are only excluding one form of society as impossible, while leaving open other possibilities (and Mosca claimed that in the social sciences it is easier to foresee *what is never going to happen*, than to foresee exactly what will happen); whereas the

Marxists are predicting that a particular form of society will necessarily come into existence. But one might equally well say that the elite theorists—and especially Pareto—are claiming that one type of political society is universal and necessary, and that the Marxists deny the universal validity of this "law of elites and masses" and assert man's liberty to imagine and create new forms of society. In short, there is in both theories an element of social determinism which may be more or less strongly emphasized.

I mention this question now only in order to bring out the connexion between the ideological and the theoretical aspects of the concept of elites. The concept refers to an observable social phenomenon and takes its place in theories which seek to explain social happenings, especially political changes. At the same time the concept makes its appearance in social thought at a time and in circumstances which at once give it an ideological significance in the contest between economic liberalism and socialism, and it spreads widely in doctrines which have an avowed ideological purpose. Even later, even in our allegedly post-ideological age, the concept cannot be regarded as a purely scientific construct; for every sociological concept and theory has an ideological force by reason of its influence upon the thoughts and actions of men in their everyday life. It may have this influence either because it is impregnated with a social doctrine, or because, while it excludes any immediate doctrinal influence, it nevertheless draws attention to and emphasizes certain features of social life and neglects others, and thus persuades men to conceive of their condition and their possible future in one set of terms rather than another. To criticize a conceptual scheme or a theory in its ideological aspect is not, therefore, simply to show its connexion with a broader doctrine of man and society and to oppose another social doctrine to it; it is also, or mainly, to show the scientific limitations of the concepts and theories, and to propose new concepts and theories which are truer or more adequate to describe what actually occurs in the sphere of society. In what follows I shall be concerned, for the most part, with just such a critical examination of the idea of elites, and only at the end of the book shall I return to a discussion of the rival social doctrines which are imperfectly expressed through the scientific theories.

## NOTES

1 See the *Dictionnaire de Trévous* (1771) where the primary meaning of *élite* is given as "Ce qu'il y a de meilleur dans chaque espèce de marchandise"; and it is then added that "ce terme a passé de la boutique des marchands à d'autres usages . . . (troupes d'élite, l'élite de la noblesse)." (Quoted in Renzo Sereno, "The Anti-Aristotelianism of Gaetano Mosca and Its Fate", *Ethics*, XLVIII (4), July, 1938, p. 515.) In the sixteenth century, according to Edmond Huguet, *Dictionnaire de la langue française du seizième siècle*, the word *élite* meant simply *choix* (a choice); *faire élite* meant "to make a choice." See also, on the early uses of the term itself and of the idea of elites, Hans P. Dreitzel, *Elitebegriff und Sozialstruktur*, and H. D. Lasswell *et al.*, *The Comparative Study of Elites*. The idea that the community should be ruled by a group of superior individuals figures prominently in Plato's thought, and even more in the Brahminical caste-doctrines which regulated ancient Indian society. In another form, which yet has an important influence upon social theories, many religious creeds have expressed the notion of an elite in terms of the "elect of God". The modern, social and political, conception of elites may perhaps be traced back to Saint-Simon's advocacy of the rule of scientists and industrialists; but in Saint-Simon's work the idea is qualified in numerous ways, and especially by his recognition of class differences and of the opposition between the rich and the poor, which allowed his immediate followers to develop his thought in the direction of socialism. It was in the positive philosophy of Auguste Comte that the elitist and authoritarian elements in Saint-Simon's thought, allied with the ideas of de Bonald, were restored to prominence, and so influenced directly the creators of the modern theory of elites, Mosca and Pareto. (Full references to the works cited in footnotes will be found in the Selected Bibliography at the end of this volume.)

2 V. Pareto, *The Mind and Society*, III, pp. 1422-3.

3 Ibid., pp. 1423-4.

4 Lausanne, 1896-7.

5 1st edn. Paris, 1902; 2nd edn. 1926.

6 Op. cit., p. 28.

7 Gaetano Mosca, *The Ruling Class*. This English version, edited by Arthur Livingston, is a conflation and rearrangement of chapters from two separate editions of Mosca's *Elementi di scienza politica* (1st edn. 1896, 2nd revised and enlarged edn. 1923). An excellent recent study of Mosca's work—J. H.

Meisel, *The Myth of the Ruling Class*—makes clear that Mosca had formulated the main elements of his doctrine in his first book, *Sulla Teorica dei governi e sul governo parlamentare: Studi storici e sociali* (Turin, 1884), and shows how this doctrine was elaborated and qualified in his later writings. Meisel also discusses with great fairness (op. cit., Chap. 8) the relation between the ideas of Mosca and Pareto and shows that the latter can hardly be convicted of simple plagiarism (as Mosca claimed); nevertheless, Pareto's later account of the governing elite does seem to owe something to Mosca's doctrine.

[8] G. Mosca, *The Ruling Class*, p. 50.

[9] Ibid., p. 53.

[10] V. Pareto, *The Mind and Society*, III, pp. 1429–30.

[11] Marie Kolabinska, *La circulation des élites en France*, p. 7.

[12] Antonio Gramsci, *Note sul Machiavelli*.

[13] Idem. From his prison diary (1932), published in *Gli Intellettuali e l'organizzazione della cultura*.

[14] Except that under the influence of democratic sentiments the governing elite is likely to be hesitant and incompetent in its rule. As so often, there is a conflict here between Pareto's science and his political doctrine; in a democratic system there is still, inevitably, a governing elite, and yet Pareto inveighs against democracy as though it were actually a real threat to the existence of such an elite.

[15] Cf. Meisel, op. cit., p. 303 "... like the Marxian classes, Mosca's social forces closely reflect all the changes, economic, social, cultural, of an evolving civilization. With every new need, new social forces rise to meet the challenge and to ask their share of power of the old established interests."

[16] Lasswell, in H. D. Lasswell, D. Lerner and C. E. Rothwell, *The Comparative Study of Elites*.

[17] Raymond Aron, "Social Structure and the Ruling Class, Part I", *British Journal of Sociology*, I (1), 1950. "The problem of combining in a synthesis 'class' sociology and 'elite' sociology ... can be reduced to the following question: 'What is the relation between social differentiation and political hierarchy in modern societies?'"

[18] See Aron, *The Opium of the Intellectuals* (London, 1957).

[19] This has also been proposed by Raymond Aron in his article, "Classe sociale, classe politique, classe dirigeante", *European Journal of Sociology*, I (2), 1960; and I follow his suggestions to some extent.

[20] Both writers insisted strongly upon the positive, scientific character of their studies, and their merits in this respect have been very favourably assessed in James Burnham's *The Machiavellians*.

[21] The critique of socialist doctrines and movements is a prominent feature of Robert Michels' *Political Parties*, which will be examined later.

[22] Carl J. Friedrich, *The New Image of the Common Man*.

[23] G. Lukács, *Die Zerstörung der Vernunft*.

[24] J. A. Schumpeter, *Capitalism, Socialism and Democracy*.

[25] Karl Mannheim, *Ideology and Utopia* (1929, English trans. 1936), p. 119.

26 Idem, *Essays on the Sociology of Culture.*

27 J. A. Schumpeter, op. cit., p. 271.

28 Raymond Williams, *Culture and Society* (Penguin Books edn.), p. 236.

29 J. H. Meisel, op. cit., p. 10.

30 M. Kolabinska, op. cit., p. 5. S. F. Nadel, in his essay on "The Concept of Social Elites", *International Social Science Bulletin* VIII (3), 1956, also emphasizes "social superiority" as the distinguishing feature of an elite, without noticing the ideological element in this conception.

## II

# FROM THE RULING CLASS TO THE POWER ELITE

THE concern which Mosca and Pareto displayed to create a new science of politics was provoked, as we have seen, by their opposition to socialism, and especially to Marx's social theory which had given to the developing labour movement a remarkable intellectual energy and self-confidence. Is this new science of the "Machiavellians," as James Burnham has called them,[1] superior to Marx's theory of social classes and class conflict?

Marx's theory may be stated briefly in the following propositions:

(1) in every society beyond the most primitive, two categories of people may be distinguished:
   (a) a ruling class, and (b) one or more subject classes.
(2) the dominant position of the ruling class is to be explained by its possession of the major instruments of economic production, but its political dominance is consolidated by the hold which it establishes over military force and over the production of ideas.
(3) there is perpetual conflict between the ruling class and the subject class or classes; and the nature and course of such conflict is influenced primarily by the development of productive forces, i.e. by changes in technology.
(4) the lines of class conflict are most sharply drawn in the modern capitalist societies, because in such societies the

divergence of economic interests appears most clearly, unobscured by any personal bonds such as those of feudal society, and because the development of capitalism brings about a more radical polarization of classes than has existed in any other type of society, by its unrivalled concentration of wealth at one extreme of society and of poverty at the other, and by its gradual elimination of the intermediate and transitional social strata.

(5) the class struggle within capitalist society will end with the victory of the working class, and this victory will be followed by the construction of a classless society. A number of reasons are advanced for expecting the advent of a classless society. First, the tendency of modern capitalism is to create a homogeneous working class, from which it is unlikely that new social divisions will spring in the future. Secondly, the revolutionary struggle of the workers itself engenders co-operation and a sentiment of brotherhood, and this sentiment is strengthened by the moral and social doctrines which the revolutionary movement produces, and which have been absorbed into Marx's own thought. Thirdly, capitalism creates the material and cultural pre-conditions for a classless society —the material conditions by its immense productivity which renders possible the satisfaction of the basic needs of all men and removes the edge from the struggle for physical survival, and the cultural conditions by overcoming the "idiocy of rural life," promoting literacy, diffusing scientific knowledge, and engaging the mass of the people in political life.

Marx's theory was the most comprehensive and systematic which had been propounded in the social sciences up to that time, and in retrospect it is not surprising that it should have dominated social thought during the past hundred years and influenced so strongly the growth of the labour movement. Nor is it surprising, on the other hand, that the boldness and range of its generalizations, and the revolutionary doctrine which claimed to be founded upon them, should have attracted so many critical refutations. The lines of criticism have been various. At one level the economic interpretation of history is attacked in very general terms, as a monocausal theory which cannot possibly do justice to the complexity of historical changes. Both Mosca and Pareto argued in this manner, but in the course of their argument they extended unjustifiably the scope of Marx's theory. Marx did not say that all social and cultural changes could be explained by economic factors. He sought to establish that the principal types of society, primarily within the area of European civilization, could be distinguished in terms of their economic systems, and that *major* social changes, from one type of society to another, could best be explained by changes in economic activity which brought into existence new social groups with new interests. A more serious criticism of Marx's theory would consist in showing that one or more of the principal types of society as defined by him came into existence, was maintained or declined by the operation of non-economic factors. This is what Schumpeter, for example, intended when he drew attention to the difficulty of explaining the rise of European feudalism by economic factors, and to the tendency of social institutions to maintain their form in changed economic circumstances: "Social structures, types and attitudes are coins that do not readily melt. Once they are formed they persist, possibly for centuries, and since different structures and types display different degrees of this ability to survive, we almost always find that actual group and national behaviour more or less departs from what we should expect it to be if we tried to infer it from the dominant forms of the productive process. Though this applies quite generally, it is most clearly seen when a highly durable structure transfers itself bodily from one country to another. ... A related case is of more ominous significance. Consider the emergence of the feudal type of landlordism in the kingdom of the Franks during the sixth and seventh centuries. This was certainly a most important event that shaped the structure of society for many ages and *also influenced conditions of production, wants and technology included*. But its simplest explanation is to be found in the function of military leadership previously filled by the families and individuals who (retaining that function however) became feudal landlords after the definitive conquest of the new territory."[2] The emergence of feudal societies, in Europe and elsewhere, does indeed constitute a difficult problem for the Marxist theory since, although these societies can be regarded as resulting immediately from a combination of traditions of military chieftainship with large-scale landownership in a settled agrarian society (and so not entirely excluded from the scope of an economic interpretation of history), nevertheless they appear primarily as political creations, which arise in response to the disintegration of centralized empires.

A still more damaging criticism of Marx's theory, along the same lines, would be one which cast doubt upon the economic interpretation of the origins of modern capitalism, i.e. upon the explanation of the very transition from one type of society to another which Marx examined in the greatest detail and which he thought provided convincing evidence for his theory. The best known of such criticisms is Max Weber's attempt to show, in *The Protestant Ethic and the Spirit of Capitalism*, that the development of modern capitalism required, besides the economic changes and the formation of a new class which Marx had postulated, a radical change in men's attitudes towards work and the accumulation of wealth, which the Protestant religion brought about. Weber introduced many qualifications into his argument—including the recognition that Protestant doctrines were mainly accepted by those social groups which were already engaged in capitalistic economic activities—but it stands none the less as an attempted refutation of Marx, in so far as it denies that the change from feudalism to capitalism was brought about solely or primarily by economic factors. But is Weber's own thesis valid? It has been criticized on various grounds: that it is historically inaccurate in its portrayal of the Protestant ethic, and in its account of the connexions between Protestantism and capitalistic enterprise; and more generally, that it does not provide an independent explanation of the rise of capitalism. In order to do this, Weber would have had to show, not merely that the Protestant ethic was a significant element in the formation of new economic attitudes, but also that no other ideas which were germinating in the circles of the *bourgeoisie* could have served the same purpose, and that the historical accident of the Reformation was therefore essential to the development of capitalism. In recent years the value of Weber's thesis has come to be more modestly assessed, as emphasizing more strongly than Marx's theory had done (in spite of Marx's analysis of utilitarianism as the ideology of the *bourgeoisie*) the importance of ideologies in accelerating or retarding social changes. At the present day, we are better able to recognize the important role of ideologies in social change, because we have the experience of the achievements of Marxism itself as an ideology which powerfully assists rapid industrialization, and on the other hand, of the retarding influence of traditional creeds in such underdeveloped countries as India.

The value of Marx's concept of the ruling class depends upon the truth of his general social theory. If that theory is not universally valid a ruling class may be conceived as originating from military power, or in modern times from the power of a political party, just as well as from the ownership of the means of production. It may still be maintained, however, that the consolidation of a ruling class requires the concentration of the various types of power—economic, military and political—and that, as a matter of fact, in most societies the formation of this class has begun with the acquisition of economic power. But this raises a more fundamental question about the idea of a ruling class. Is it the case that in every society other than the most simple and primitive this concentration of power occurs, that a ruling class is formed? It should be said at once that the different types of society conform in varying degrees with Marx's model of a society which is clearly divided between a ruling class and subject classes. The most favourable case is probably that of European feudalism, characterized by the rule of a warrior class[3] which had securely in its hands the ownership of land, military force, and political authority, and which received the ideological support of a powerful Church. But even here, a number of qualifications are necessary. The idea of a cohesive ruling class is contradicted by the decentralization of political power which was characteristic of feudal societies,[4] and at the stage when this decentralization was overcome—in the absolute monarchies—the European societies were no longer ruled, in a strict sense, by a warrior nobility. Nevertheless, the nobility of the *ancien régime* does come close to the ideal type of a ruling class.

Another case which fits Marx's model well in many respects is that of the *bourgeoisie* of early capitalism. The development of the *bourgeoisie* as an important social class can well be explained by economic changes, and its rise in the economic sphere was accompanied by the acquisition of other positions of power and prestige in society—in politics, administration, the armed forces and the educational system.

This conquest of power in the different spheres of society was a long and confused process, which had many local variations in the European countries, and Marx's model was an abstraction from the complex historical reality, bringing together the experiences of the revolution in France—the most violent ideological and political expression of the rise of a new class—and those of the industrial revolution in England. Nevertheless, the pattern of events does conform broadly with Marx's scheme; in England, the Reform Act of 1832 gave political power to the *bourgeoisie*, and it produced changes in the character of legislation even if it did not, for some considerable time, change the social composition of Parliament or cabinets[5]; the reform of the Civil Service after 1855 opened the way for upper middle class aspirants to the highest administrative posts[6]; and the development of public schools created new opportunities for children from the newly rich industrial and commercial families to be trained for elite positions. The *bourgeoisie* also gained powerful ideological support, according to Marx's account, from the political economists and the utilitarian philosophers.

Nevertheless, the bourgeoisie appears in several respects a less cohesive ruling class than the feudal nobility. It does not actually combine in the same persons military, political and economic power, and there arises the possibility of conflicts of interest between the different groups which *represent* (as Marx says) the *bourgeoisie*. Furthermore, capitalist society is more open and mobile than was feudal society, and in the ideological sphere especially, with the development of secular intellectual occupations, conflicting doctrines may arise. Marx expected that the polarization of the two principal classes—the *bourgeoisie* and industrial working class—would accompany the development of capitalism, and that the rule of the *bourgeoisie* would become more manifest and more onerous. But this did not happen in the advanced capitalist societies: the different spheres of power appear to have become more distinct, and the sources of power more numerous and varied; the opposition between the "two great classes" of Marx's theory has been modified by the growth of the new middle classes and by a much more complex differentiation of occupation and status; and political rule has become altogether more mild and less repressive. One important element in this development has been the introduction of universal adult suffrage, which produces, in principle, a separation between economic and political power. Marx himself considered that the attainment of universal suffrage would be a *revolutionary* step, and that it would transfer political power to the working class.[7] Thus, whereas the connexion between economic and political power can easily be established in the case of feudal society, or in the case of early capitalism with its limitation of political rights to property owners, it cannot be so easily established in the case of the modern capitalist democracies, and the notion of a distinct and settled ruling class becomes dubious and unclear. Marxist fundamentalists, in their attempts to preserve Marx's social theory intact, have been obliged to argue that even in political democracies the *bourgeoisie always* effectively rules through the indirect influence of wealth, but this is more easily asserted than demonstrated.

These, in brief, are some of the principal difficulties in Marx's conception of the ruling class. Its value lies in the rigorous attempt to analyse the sources of political power, and to explain major changes of political regime. With the aid of this conception Marx succeeded in expressing in a more exact form an idea which recurs continually in popular thought and in social theory: namely, that one of the principal structural features of human societies is their division into a ruling and exploiting group on one side, and subject, exploited groups on the other[8]; in providing an explanation of the causes of this division by connecting in an impressive synthesis a mass of hitherto unrelated economic, political and cultural facts; and in accounting for changes in social structure by the rise and fall of classes. The concept of the "governing elite" or "political class" was proposed as an alternative, partly, as we have seen, in order to demonstrate the impossibility of attaining a classless form of society, but also to meet the theoretical difficulties which we have just considered. The concept of a governing elite avoids, in particular, the difficulty of showing that a particular class, defined in terms of its economic position, does in fact dominate all the spheres of social life; but it does so only at the cost of abandoning any attempt to explain the phenomena to which it refers. The governing elite, according to Mosca and Pareto, comprises those who occupy the recognized positions of political power in a society. Thus, when we ask, who has power in a particular society, the reply is, those who have power, i.e. those who occupy the specified positions. This is scarcely illuminating; it does not tell us how these particular individuals come to occupy the positions of power. Or else it is misleading; if, for example, those who appear to have power in the formal system of government are in fact subject to the power of other individuals or groups outside this system. Nor does this idea of a governing elite provide much help in the explanation of political changes. Pareto's theory of the circulation of elites, which we shall examine in the next chapter, rests upon assertions about the distribution of psychological characteristics in a population which present numerous difficulties and which remain untested in Pareto's own work. Mosca, on the other hand, when he turns to consider the problems of political change, has to introduce the notion of "social forces" (i.e. important interests in society) as the source of new elites; and as Meisel has commented, this brings him "uncomfortably close to Marx."[9]

The difficulties in the concept of a governing elite can be seen most clearly in a recent work which shows the influence of Marx on one side and of Mosca and Pareto on the other —the late C. Wright Mills' *The Power Elite*. Mills explains his preference for the term "power elite" rather than "ruling class" by saying: " 'Ruling class' is a badly loaded phrase. 'Class' is an economic term; 'rule' a political one. The phrase 'ruling class,' thus contains the theory that an economic class rules politically. That short-cut theory may or may not at times be true, but we do not want to carry that one rather simple theory about in the terms that we use to define our problems; we wish to state the theories explicitly, using terms of more precise and unilateral meaning. Specifically, the phrase 'ruling class,' in its common political connotations, does not allow enough autonomy to the political order and its agents, and it says nothing about the military as such . . . We hold that such a simple view of 'economic determinism' must be elaborated by 'political determinism' and 'military determinism'; that the higher agents of each of these three domains now often have a noticeable degree of autonomy; and that only in the often intricate ways of coalition do they make up and carry through the most important decisions."[10]

Mills defines the power elite in much the same way as Pareto defined his "governing elite," for he says "we may define the power elite in terms of the means of power—as those who occupy the command posts."[11] But the analysis which proceeds from this definition has a number of unsatisfactory features. In the first place, Mills distinguishes three major elites in the USA—the corporation heads, the political leaders and the military chiefs—and he is obliged to go on to inquire whether these three groups together form a single power elite, and if so, what it is that binds them together. One possible answer to these questions is to say that the three groups do form a single elite because they are representatives of an upper class, which has to be regarded, consequently, as a ruling class. But Mills, although he emphasizes that most of the members of these elites are in fact drawn from a socially recognized upper class, says initially that he will leave open the question of whether or not it is such a class which rules through the elites, and when he returns to the problem it is only to reject the Marxist idea of a ruling class in the brief passage cited above. In short, the question is never seriously discussed, and this is a curious failing in the particular case which Mills is examining, and in the context of the ideas which he is expressing. He has previously rejected the view that there is popular control of the power elite through voting or other means, and has emphasized the unity of the elite, as well as the homogeneity of its social origins—all of which points to the consolidation of a ruling class. The formulation which he actually gives is vague and unconvincing: it is a reference to "the often uneasy coincidence of economic, military, and political power," a coincidence which he proposes to explain largely by the pressures of the international conflict in which America has been engaged.

These problems have frequently been raised in criticisms of Mosca and Pareto. Thus, Carl J. Friedrich observed that one of the most problematical parts of all elite doctrines is the assumption that the men of power do constitute a cohesive group: "In the light of the continuous change in the composition of the majority, it is not possible to say, under conditions such as prevail in a functioning democracy, that those who play some considerable part in government constitute a cohesive group."[12] This view of the elite in modern democracies has been widely held; it is stated boldly in the conclusions of a recent study of the upper strata of British society:

". . . the rulers are not at all close-knit or united. They are not so much in the centre of a solar system, as in a cluster of interlocking circles, each one largely preoccupied with its own professionalism and expertise, and touching others only at one edge . . . they are not a single Establishment but a ring of Establishments, with slender connexions. The frictions and balances between the different circles are the supreme safeguard of democracy. No one man can stand in the centre, for there is no centre."[13]

Mills rejects this fashionable liberal-minded doctrine, which he summarizes as follows: "Far from being omnipotent, the elites are thought to be so scattered as to lack any coherence as a historical force . . . Those who occupy the formal places of authority are so checkmated—by other elites exerting pressure, or by the public as an electorate, or by constitutional codes—that although there may be upper classes, there is no ruling class; although there may be men of power, there is no power elite; although there may be a system of stratification, it has no effective top."[14] As we have seen, he insists that the three principal elites—economic, political and military—are, in fact, a cohesive group, and he supports his view by establishing the similarity of their social origins, the close personal and family relationships between those in the different elites, and the frequency of interchange of personnel between the three spheres. But since he resists the conclusion that the group is a ruling class he is unable to provide a convincing explanation, as distinct from description, of the solidarity of the power elite. Furthermore, by eliminating the idea of a ruling class, he also excludes that of classes in opposition; and so he arrives at an extremely pessimistic account of American society. The real themes of his book are, first, the transformation of a society in which numerous small and autonomous groups had an effective say in the making of political decisions, into a mass society in which the power elite decides all important issues and keeps the masses quiet by flattery, deception and entertainment; and secondly, the corruption of the power elite itself, which he attributes primarily to a state of affairs in which it is not accountable for its decisions to any organized public, and also to the dominant value of the acquisition of wealth. Mills' account of the historical changes, which does indeed bring to light some important features of modern politics—the growing political influence of military chiefs, for example— is pessimistic in the sense that it suggests no way out of the situation which it describes and condemns. Like Pareto and Mosca, Mills seems to be saying that if we look at modern societies without illusions we shall see that, however democratic their constitutions, they are in fact ruled by an elite; and to be adding, in a devastating fashion, that even in a society so favourably placed as was the USA at its origins— without a feudal system of ranks, with very considerable equality of economic and social condition among its citizens, and with a strongly democratic ideology—the force of events has produced a governing elite of unprecedented power and unaccountability. Where Mills differs from the other Machiavellians is in condemning a state of affairs which they either praised or, in a spirit of disillusionment, accepted.

The concepts of "ruling class" and "governing elite" are used in descriptions and explanations of political happenings, and their value must be judged by the extent to which they make possible reasonable answers to important questions about political systems. Do the rulers of society constitute a social group? Is it a cohesive or divided, an open or closed group? How are its members selected? What is the basis of their power? Is this power unrestricted or is it limited by that of other groups in society? Are there significant and regular differences between societies in these respects, and if so, how are they to be explained?

The two concepts are alike in emphasizing the division between rulers and ruled as one of the most important facts of social structure.[15] But they state the division in different ways: the concept of a "governing elite" contrasts the organized, ruling minority with the unorganized majority, or masses, while the concept of a "ruling class" contrasts the dominant class with subject classes, which may themselves be organized, or be creating organizations. From these different conceptions arise differences in the way of conceiving the relations between rulers and ruled. In the Marxist theory, which employs the concept of a ruling class, the conflict between classes becomes the principal force producing changes of social structure; but in the elite theories—in spite of the fact that Pareto praised highly Marx's conception of class struggle, which he described as "profoundly true,"[16] —the relations between the organized minority and the unorganized majority are necessarily represented as more passive, and the resulting problem of how to explain the rise and fall of ruling elites, if it is confronted at all, has to be dealt with either by postulating a recurrent decadence in the elite (Pareto) or by introducing the idea of the rise of new "social forces" among the masses (Mosca) which brings the theory close to Marxism.

A further difference between the two concepts lies in the extent to which they make possible explanations of the cohesion of the ruling minority. The "governing elite," defined as those who occupy the positions of command in a society, is merely assumed to be a cohesive group, unless other considerations, such as their membership of the wealthy class, or their aristocratic family origins are introduced (as they are consistently by Mosca, and occasionally by Pareto). But the "ruling class," defined as the class which owns the major instruments of economic production in a society, is shown to be a cohesive social group; first, because its members have definite economic interests in common, and, more importantly, because it is engaged permanently in a conflict with other classes in society, through which its self-awareness and solidarity are continually enhanced. Furthermore, this concept states in a precise form what is the basis of the minority's ruling position, namely its economic dominance, while the concept of the "governing elite" says little about the bases of the power which the elite possesses, except in so far as it incorporates elements from the Marxist theory of classes. In Mills' study of the "power elite," there is an attempt to explain the power position of the three principal elites taken separately—that of the business executives by the growth in size and complexity of business corporations; that of the military chiefs by the growing scale and expense of the weapons of war, determined by technology and the state of international conflict; and that of the national political leaders, in a somewhat less satisfactory way, by the decline of the legislature, of local politics and of voluntary organizations—but the unity of the power elite as a single group, and the basis of *its* power, are not explained. Why is there *one* power elite and not *three*?

The superiority of the concept of "ruling class" lies in its greater fertility and suggestiveness and in its value in the construction of theories. But I have pointed out earlier some of its defects, and it is now necessary to consider whether these can be overcome. The most important step in this direction would be to give up the Marxist view of the concept as a description of a real phenomenon which is to be observed in all societies in the same general form, and to regard it instead as an "ideal type," in the sense which Max Weber gave to this term.[17] If we treat the concept in this way we can proceed to ask how closely the relationships in a particular society approach the ideal type of a ruling class and subject classes; and so employ the concept, properly, as a tool of thought and investigation. It is then possible to see clearly that the idea of a "ruling class" originated in the study of a particular historical situation—the end of feudalism and the beginnings of modern capitalism[18]—and to consider how far, and in what respects, other situations diverge from this ideal type, as a result of the absence or weakness of class formation, the influence of factors other than the ownership of property in the creation of classes, and the conflict between different forms of power.

There are two sorts of situation in which we can see especially plainly a divergence from the ideal type of a ruling class. One is that in which, although there is an "upper class" —that is to say, a clearly demarcated social group which has in its possession a large part of the property of society and re-ceives a disproportionately large share of the national income, and which has created on the basis of these economic advan-tages a distinctive culture and way of life—this class does not enjoy undisputed or unrestricted political power, in the sense that it is able to maintain easily its property rights or to transmit them unimpaired from generation to generation. This kind of situation has been discerned by many observers particularly in the modern democracies, in which, as I noted earlier, there is a potential opposition between the ownership of wealth and productive resources by a small upper class, and the possession of political power, through the franchise, by the mass of the population. As de Tocqueville once wrote: "Il est contradictoire que le peuple soit à la fois misérable et souverain."

In order to determine whether in such a case there is a "ruling class" it is necessary first to examine the degree in which the upper class has been successful in perpetuating its ownership of property. We shall have to note, on one side, that in the democratic countries during the present century a considerable number of restrictions have been placed upon the use of private property, and that there has probably been some reduction in the inequalities of wealth and income, as a result of progressive taxation, and of the growth of publicly owned property and publicly administered social services. On the other side we must note that the decline in the proportion of private wealth owned by the upper class has been modest and very slow, and that the redistribution of income through taxation has not proceeded very far. The situation in Britain was very carefully examined by John Strachey,[19] who concluded that "up to 1939 there had been little or no redistribution of the national income in favour of the mass of the population, either through trade union pressure or budgetary changes . . . the wage earners' standard of life had risen just about in step with the rise in the total national income, their share remaining about constant . . . the broad pattern of distribution which emerges . . . is that at the end of the period under discussion [1939] as at the beginning [1911] some 10 per cent of the population got nearly one-half of the national income and the other 90 per cent got the other half of the national income."[20] In the following period, up to 1951, there was some redistribution of income which resulted in transferring some 10 per cent of the total national income from property owners to wage-earners, but this trend was probably reversed again after 1951.[21] Strachey concludes: "All this is evidence that capitalism has in fact an innate tendency to extreme and ever-growing inequality. For how otherwise could all these cumulatively equalitarian measures which the popular forces have succeeded in enacting over the past hundred years have done little more than hold the position constant? Is it not clear that, if the workings of the system had not been continuously modified, it would have produced just that ever sharper polarization which Marx diagnosed as its essential tendency?"[22] It is evidence, to put the matter in another way, that the upper class in Britain has been able to resist with considerable success the attacks upon its economic interests, and that in this sense of having the power to defend its interests it has maintained itself during the present century as a ruling class. The situation in the other democratic countries, with the exception of the Scandinavian countries, does not differ greatly from that in Britain; in all of them, right-wing governments have been in power during most of the present century and the redistribution of wealth and income has occurred slowly, if at all. One must be sceptical, therefore, of the view that the extension of voting rights to the mass of the population can establish at once—or has in fact established in the short period of time in which modern democracies have existed—popular rule, and eliminate the power of a ruling class. What seems to have taken place in the democratic countries up to the present time is not so much a reduction in the power of the upper class as a decline in the radicalism of the working class.

The second type of situation in which there is a divergence from the "ruling class—subject classes" model is that in which the ruling group is not a class in Marx's sense. One instance is provided by those societies in which a stratum of intellectuals or bureaucrats may be said to wield supreme power—in China under the rule of the *literati*, or in India under the rule of the Brahmins. Another instance is to be found in the present-day Communist countries where power is concentrated in the leaders of a political party. In these cases, however, we need to examine carefully how far the ruling stratum is clearly distinguishable from a ruling class. In India, the Brahmins, during the ages when they were most powerful, were also substantial landowners, and they were closely allied with the landowning warrior castes in the imperial and feudal periods of India's history. On occasion, they themselves founded ruling or noble houses, and there seems to have been, at times, an amount of movement of individuals and families between the Brahmin and Kshatriya (warrior) castes, which the doctrines of caste exclusiveness expounded in the classical texts do not indicate.

Again, in China, the *literati* were recruited, in the feudal period, from the principal landowning families, and at other times they came in the main from wealthy families[23]; so that they were always closely linked with an upper class. There is, moreover, another important economic aspect of the rule of these groups of intellectuals and administrators to which Karl Wittfogel has drawn attention.[24] One of the principal instruments of production in China and India (and in a number of other ancient societies)[25] was the system of irrigation, and the *literati* and the Brahmins, without owning this property upon which agricultural production depended, still exercised a more or less complete control over its use. Consequently they possessed, in addition to their ownership of land, a vital economic power which, according to Wittfogel, was the principal support of their political dominance.

But notwithstanding these qualifications the distinction between social strata of this kind and ruling classes which base their power directly upon the legal ownership of property remains. The possession of the means of administration may be, as Max Weber argued, an alternative to the possession of means of economic production, as a basis of political power.[26] This distinction is perhaps more obvious in the case of the present-day Communist countries, in which there is no private ownership of the means of production, and in which the officials of the ruling party and the state control the economy. Wittfogel has attempted, in a very ingenious way, to assimilate this type of political power to the general category of "oriental despotism"[27] but I think the differences are too great—the existence of private ownership of land and other resources, and the intimate bonds between the officials and the property-owning classes in one case, and the specific characteristics of rule by a political party in the other[28]—for this attempt to be successful. The political system of the Communist countries seems to me to approach the pure type of a "power elite," that is, a group which, having come to power with the support or acquiescence of particular classes in the population, maintains itself in power chiefly by virtue of being an organized minority confronting the unorganized majority; whereas in the case of ancient China or India we have to deal with a system which combines the features of a ruling class and a power elite.

There is another element in the position of a ruling class, which has already been mentioned and which needs to be examined more fully in its bearing upon those situations in which the existence of such a class is doubtful. Since the power of a ruling class arises from its ownership of property, and since this property can easily be transmitted from generation to generation, the class has an enduring character. It is constituted by a group of families which remain as its component elements over long periods of time through the transmission of the family property. Its composition is not entirely immutable, for new families may enter it and old families may decline, but the greater part of its members continue from generation to generation. Only when there are rapid changes in the whole system of production and property ownership does the composition of the ruling class change significantly; and in that case we can say that one ruling class has been replaced by another. If, however, we were to find, in a particular society or type of society, that the movement of individuals and families between the different social levels was so continuous and so extensive that no group of families was able to maintain itself for any length of time in a situation of economic and political pre-eminence, then we should have to say that in such a society there was no ruling class. It is, in fact, this "circulation of elites" (in the terminology of the elite theorists) or "social mobility" (in the language of more recent sociological studies) that has been fixed upon by a number of writers as a second important characteristic of modern industrial societies—the first being universal suffrage—which must qualify severely, if it does not altogether exclude, the assertion that there is a ruling class in these societies. By this means we may arrive at the view, which was formulated by Karl Mannheim among others,[29] that the development of industrial societies can properly be depicted as a movement from a class system to a system of elites, from a social hierarchy based upon the inheritance of property to one based upon merit and achievement.

This confrontation between the concepts of "ruling class" and "political elite" shows, I think, that, while on one level they may be totally opposed, as elements in wide-ranging theories which interpret political life, and especially the future possibilities of political organization, in very different ways, on another level they may be seen as complementary concepts, which refer to different types of political system or to different aspects of the same political system. With their help we can attempt to distinguish between societies in which there is a ruling class, and at the same time elites which represent particular aspects of its interests; societies in which there is no ruling class, but a political elite which founds its power upon the control of the administration, or upon military force, rather than upon property ownership and inheritance; and societies in which there exists a multiplicity of elites among which no cohesive and enduring group of powerful individuals or families seems to be discoverable at all. In order to establish such a classification we need to examine more closely

—as I shall do in the following chapters—the circulation of elites, the relations between elites and classes, and the ways in which new elites and new classes are formed.

## NOTES

1 James Burnham, *The Machiavellians*.

2 J. A. Schumpeter, *Capitalism, Socialism and Democracy*, pp. 12–13.

3 See Marc Bloch, *Feudal Society*, Vol. II, Book III, Chap. I.

4 Marc Bloch, op. cit.

5 See W. L. Guttsman, *The British Political Elite*, Chap. 3, "The changing social structure of the British political elite: 1868–1955."

6 See J. Donald Kingsley, *Representative Bureaucracy*, especially Chap. III, "Middle Class Reform: the Triumph of Plutocracy." Kingsley concludes that "the middle classes had by 1870 destroyed the *ancien régime* on almost every front, [but] the chief gains had been made by the upper ranks of those classes. In the House of Commons wealthy merchants, bankers, industrialists, were displacing the landlords and would begin before many years to replace them in the cabinet. In the Civil Service a somewhat comparable change had occurred. Entrance to the higher posts was no longer a matter of aristocratic influence. The key that now unlocked the door was a costly education which . . . gave to the new system a 'plutocratic character' " (p. 76).

7 Karl Marx, "The Chartists", *New York Daily Tribune*, 25th August 1852. "We now come to the *Chartists*, the politically active portion of the British *working class*. The six points of the Charter which they contend for contain nothing but the demand of *Universal Suffrage*, and of the conditions without which Universal Suffrage would be illusory for the working class; such as the ballot, payment of members, annual general elections. But Universal Suffrage is the equivalent of political power for the working class of England, where the proletariat forms the large majority of the population, where, in a long, though underground civil war, it has gained a clear consciousness of its position as a class, and where even the rural districts know no longer any peasants, but only landlords, industrial capitalists (farmers) and hired labourers. The carrying of Universal Suffrage in England would, therefore, be a far more socialistic measure than anything which has been honoured with that name on the Continent. Its inevitable result, here, is *the political supremacy of the working class.*"

8 Cf. Stanislaw Ossowski, *Class Structure in the Social Consciousness*, Chap. II.

9 J. H. Meisel, op. cit.

10 op. cit., p. 277.

11 op. cit., p. 23.

12 Carl J. Friedrich, *The New Image of the Common Man*, pp. 259–60.

13 Anthony Sampson, *Anatomy of Britain*, p. 624.

14 op. cit., pp. 16–17.

15 "From the point of view of scientific research the real superiority of the

concept of the ruling, or political, class ['political elite' in our terminology. TBB] lies in the fact that the varying structure of ruling classes has a preponderant importance in determining the political type, and also the level of civilization, of the different peoples". Mosca, op. cit., p. 51.

[16] Pareto, *Les systèmes socialistes*, II, p. 405.

[17] An ideal type concept "brings together certain relationships and events of historical life into a complex which is conceived as an internally consistent system . . . this construction itself is like a *utopia* which has been arrived at by the analytical accentuation of certain elements of reality . . . it *is* no hypothesis but it offers guidance in the construction of hypotheses. It is not a *description* of reality but it aims to give unambiguous means of expression to such a description . . . An ideal type is formed by the one-sided *accentuation* of one or more points of view and by the synthesis of a great many diffuse, discrete, more or less present and occasionally absent *concrete individual* phenomena, which are arranged according to those one-sidedly emphasized viewpoints into a unified *analytical* construct". Max Weber, *The Methodology of the Social Sciences*, p. 90.

[18] As Croce observed of the whole theory of historical materialism: "The materialistic view of history arose out of the need to account for a definite social phenomenon, not from an abstract inquiry into the factors of historical life". B. Croce, *Historical Materialism and the Economics of Karl Marx*, p. 17.

[19] John Strachey, *Contemporary Capitalism*, Chap. VIII, "The Real Development". Strachey draws upon a number of other studies, including Douglas Jay, *The Socialist Case*; and Dudley Seers, *The Levelling of Incomes since 1938* and *Has the Distribution of Income Become More Unequal?*

[20] op. cit., pp. 137–8.

[21] Ibid., p. 146. More recently, Richard M. Titmuss, in his *Income Distribution and Social Change*, has undertaken the most thorough study yet made in Britain of the sources of information about the distribution of income. The chief purpose of his study is to inquire into the adequacy of the data which have been used by students of national income and which are derived mainly from reports and studies by the Board of Inland Revenue; and he shows in detail how inadequate they are to determine with any precision the distribution of income at a given time or its changes over time. Nevertheless, the additional factors which in his view need to be taken into account, especially in estimating the wealth and income which accrues to the upper class—life assurances, superannuation, tax-free lump sums on retirement, education covenants, discretionary trusts, expense accounts, and capital gains—work in the main to increase inequality, and a study of their magnitude suggests that any movement towards greater equality of income or wealth, since 1938, has been, to say the least, of modest dimensions. Titmuss himself concludes that " . . . we should be much more hesitant in suggesting that any equalizing forces at work in Britain since 1938 can be promoted to the status of a 'natural law' and projected into the future. As we have shown, there are often forces, deeply rooted in the social structure and fed by many complex institutional factors inherent in large-scale economies, operating in reverse directions. Some of the more critical of these factors, closely linked with the distribution of power, and containing within themselves the seeds of long-lasting effects—as, for instance, in the case of settlements and trusts—function as concealed multipliers of

inequality. They are not measured at present by the statistics of income and only marginally by the statistics of wealth. Even so, there is more than a hint from a number of studies that income inequality has been increasing since 1949 whilst the ownership of wealth, which is far more highly concentrated in the United Kingdom than in the United States, has probably become still more unequal and, in terms of family ownership, possibly strikingly more unequal, in recent years" (p. 198).

[22] Strachey, op. cit., pp. 150–1.

[23] See below, p. 65.

[24] Karl Wittfogel, *Oriental Despotism*.

[25] See Julian H. Steward *et al.*, *Irrigation Civilizations: A Comparative Study*.

[26] The characteristics of bureaucratic societies have been examined at length in a recent study: S. N. Eisenstadt, *The Political Systems of Empires*.

[27] Wittfogel, op. cit.

[28] This is discussed further in a later chapter; see pp. 77–80 below.

[29] See especially, *Man and Society*, Part II, Chap. II.

III

# POLITICS AND THE CIRCULATION OF ELITES

"HISTORY is a graveyard of aristocracies." In this graphic phrase, Pareto formulates one of the fundamental ideas of his political theory—the "circulation of elites." But in Pareto's major works the analysis of the phenomenon is less impressive than the glamour of the style. There are two principal difficulties to be confronted. In the first place, does the "circulation of elites" refer to a process in which *individuals* circulate between the elite and the non-elite, or to a process in which *one elite* is replaced by another? Both conceptions are to be found in Pareto's work, although the former predominates. When, for example, he discusses the decay and renewal of aristocracies, he observes that "the governing class is restored not only in numbers but—and that is the more important thing—in quality, by families rising from the lower classes ..."[1] Pareto refers again and again to this phenomenon, using similar expressions—"the circulation of individuals between the two strata (elite and non-elite)" (op. cit., III, p. 1427); "in the higher stratum of society, Class II residues gradually lose in strength, until now and again they are reinforced by tides upwelling from the lower stratum" (ibid.). At the same time, Pareto refers to another kind of social movement which is of vital importance for the equilibrium of society, and which consists in the emergence and rise to power of new elites. He appears to connect this movement with a failure of circulation in the first sense,

42

but it is evident that he also regards it as an aspect of the circulation of elites in general. In *Les systèmes socialistes* he observes that "a slowing down of this circulation [of individuals] may result in a considerable increase of the degenerate elements in the classes which still hold power, and on the other hand, in an increase of elements of superior quality in the subject classes. In such a case, the social equilibrium becomes unstable ... and the slightest shock will destroy it. A conquest or a revolution produces an upheaval, brings a new elite to power, and establishes a new equilibrium ..." (p. 30).

The various types of circulation of elites were differentiated more precisely by one of Pareto's pupils, Marie Kolabinska, in a work entitled *La circulation des élites en France* which was cited with approbation by the master himself. Kolabinska distinguishes three types of circulation. There is, first, the circulation which takes place between different categories of the governing elite itself. Secondly, there is the circulation between the elite and the rest of the population, which may take either of two forms: (i) individuals from the lower strata may succeed in entering the existing elite, or (ii) individuals in the lower strata may form new elite groups which then engage in a struggle for power with the existing elite. The major part of Kolabinska's work is devoted to a study of these last two processes in French society in the period between the eleventh and the eighteenth centuries, and I shall consider its findings later on.

The second difficulty in Pareto's exposition concerns his explanation of the circulation of elites. On some occasions he seems to regard elites as representing particular social interests, and the circulation of elites as resulting from the decline of established interests and the rise of new interests. Thus, he observes that "in the beginning, military, religious, and commercial aristocracies and plutocracies—with a few exceptions not worth considering—must have constituted parts of the governing elite and sometimes have made up the whole of it ..." (*The Mind and Society*, III, p. 1430). Elsewhere, in discussing the rise of new elites, he notes that the industrial workers in England have produced a trade union elite (*Les systèmes socialistes*, pp. 32–3). This type of explanation is set out more explicitly by Kolabinska, who cites as examples of rising elite groups in different periods of French history, the commercial classes, the industrial classes, the *bourgeoisie*, lawyers, and financiers.

It is clear, however, that Pareto intends to explain the circulation of elites mainly by the changes in the psychological characteristics of members of the elite on one side, and of the lower strata on the other; or, as he puts it, by the changes in the residues occurring within the two strata. Aristocracies, he says, do not decline only in numbers: "They decay also in quality, in the sense that they lose their vigour, that there is a decline in the proportions of the residues which enabled them to win their power and hold it. The governing class is restored ... by families rising from the lower classes" (*The Mind and Society*, III, p. 1430). Again, in discussing the circulation of whole groups, Pareto suggests that revolutions come about through the accumulation of decadent elements in the higher strata of society, and the increase of elements of superior quality in the lower strata (ibid., p. 1431). In order to assess the value of this explanation it is necessary to consider briefly Pareto's concept of "residues." In *The Mind and Society* he begins by making a distinction between the logical and non-logical actions ("rational" and "non-rational" would be more suitable terms) of individuals in social life: logical actions are those directed to attainable ends and employing means which are appropriate to the attainment of the ends; non-logical actions are those not directed to any end, or directed to unattainable ends, or using means which cannot attain the end. Pareto takes the view that most human actions are non-logical,[2] and he goes on to inquire what are the forces behind non-logical action and how it comes to be represented, as frequently happens, as logical action. These forces he discovers in six "residues," which he calls residues of combinations (I), of the persistence of aggregates (II), of sociability (III), of activity (IV), of the integrity of the individual (V) and of sex (VI). The ways in which the actions determined by these residues assume the appearance of logical actions are discussed by Pareto under the heading of "derivations," which bear some resemblance to "ideologies" in Marx's sense. Pareto does not define the residues very precisely, and he uses them capriciously in his descriptions of social events.[3] In the final section of *The Mind and Society*, when he treats more comprehensively the problem of the circulation of elites, he makes use of only the first two classes of residues. The rule of the governing elite, he argues, may be of two kinds: it may be maintained either by cunning (predominance of residues of combination) or by force (predominance of residues of the persistence of aggregates). Residues I and II are thus treated as categories within which all political attitudes can be classified, and the greater part of Pareto's discussion of political life amounts to an attempt to fit selected data of the history of Western societies into this scheme. It is a remarkably simple classification, especially when considered in relation to the huge edifice of concepts which Pareto has constructed in the earlier parts of his treatise; and it hardly shows any striking originality. Pareto's two types of elite, animated by residues I and II respectively —types which he also refers to as the "speculators" and the "rentiers"—bear a close resemblance to Machiavelli's "foxes" and "lions," but they are dressed up in a more scientific garb. Whether they are actually more scientific terms is open to doubt, for while there is a great parade of scientific method throughout Pareto's treatise, little or no attempt is made to establish by exact methods of investigation that the two kinds of personality which are alleged to determine the characteristics of these types of elite actually exist, or to describe them precisely in psychological terms, or to show that there are no other varieties of political personality. Even if the existence of such personality types, and their significance in political life, were assumed, it would still be necessary to show that the changes in states of mind and feeling, in ideas and sentiments, among the members of the elite are produced independently of social changes, and in turn produce the circulation of elites. This Pareto does not attempt to do; instead, he takes historical examples of declining elites and then simply asserts that there has been a change in their "residues."

Pareto's study of the rise and decline of elites as such is equally unsatisfactory. He does not attempt to assemble all the available instances (even for limited periods) and to show that there are regularities in elite circulation which might be connected with changes in sentiments, supposing that the latter could be independently established. He produces only historical illustrations, drawn mainly from contemporary Italian politics and from the history of ancient Rome, to support his general arguments.

Lastly, Pareto does not resolve the question of how the two types of elite circulation—the ascent and descent of individuals, and the rise and fall of social groups—are connected with each other. He suggests, briefly, that if the governing elite is relatively open to superior individuals from the lower strata it has a better chance of enduring,[4] and conversely, that the replacement of one elite by another may result from a failure in this circulation of individuals. Thus, he claims: "Revolutions come about through accumulations in the higher strata of society—either because of a slowing down in class circulation, or from other causes—of decadent elements no longer possessing the residues suitable for keeping them in power, or shrinking from the use of force; while meantime in the lower strata of society elements of superior quality are coming to the fore, possessing residues suitable for exercising the functions of government and willing enough to use force" (*The Mind and Society*, III, p. 1431). The reader will look in vain, however, for substantial evidence in support of these propositions, either from a comparative study of revolutions, or from a systematic comparison between societies which show important differences in the degree of circulation of individuals between the elite and the non-elite.

It is true that the data for such comparisons would be difficult to assemble, but there are historical examples which appear at once to invalidate Pareto's generalization. One such instance is that of India—a society which had, over long periods, an extremely rigid form of stratification and, so far as can be discovered, relatively little movement of individuals from the lower strata of society into the elite; but which yet experienced until modern times few revolutionary movements, and none which resulted in the replacement of one elite by another. Even if we concede that in modern Western societies it may be useful to look for a connexion between the amount of social mobility and the prevalence of revolutionary sentiments and activities, it is still not possible to explain the rise and fall of elites, whether this occurs through revolutionary or through more gradual changes, solely by the restrictions upon the movement of individuals into the elite. It is necessary to examine some of those "other causes" which Pareto mentions but does not investigate.

The work of Marie Kolabinska on elites in France was intended to demonstrate the truth of Pareto's theory by a closer study of the process of circulation in a single society. In fact, however, it provides no empirical evidence more convincing than that which Pareto's own excursions into history supply, for it employs the same inadequate method of historical illustration. For each of the periods of French history which she surveys Kolabinska cites examples of the rise or fall of particular individuals or families, but although this reveals that *some* individuals were able to change their social rank in French society during these times (and who doubted it?) it tells us nothing about the extent of such circulation, and it cannot therefore enable us to relate the volume of circulation to significant changes in the economic or political system. Only in dealing with the final period (1715–89) covered by her study does she provide any quantitative indications concerning the representation of different social strata in the elites; and even then the material which she assembles is very slight and is interpreted in a way which arouses doubts as to its significance. Thus, she quotes at one point (p. 93) a remark that in 1787 one-fifth of the higher cavalry officers did not belong to the titled nobility and that some of them did not even have the nobiliary particle "*de*" in their names, as evidence that commoners were gaining access to the military elite; yet in the very next chapter she suggests that the French elites, including the military elite, were becoming more exclusive in the years immediately preceding the Revolution, and she cites another author to the effect that the absence of the nobiliary particle was no proof at all that an individual was of non-noble birth (p. 104). It may be noted, further, that Kolabinska, who made her investigation before the publication of The Mind and Society, was fortunately dispensed from the obligation to explore the connexion between the fortunes of those individuals whose careers she traces, and their "residues," and her explanation of these movements is therefore given largely in terms of the development of new economic interests.

★ ★ ★

The same phenomena of elite circulation have been studied by a number of other writers to whose work we can turn for alternative accounts of how and why it occurs. Mosca described it in the following terms in his earliest book: "When the aptitude to command and to exercise political control is no longer the sole possession of the legal rulers but has become common enough among other people; when outside the ruling class another class has formed which finds itself deprived of power though it does have the capacity to share in the responsibilities of government—then that law has become an obstacle in the path of an elemental force and must, by one way or another, go" (*Teorica dei governi e governo parlementare*). The same idea is formulated again in his later work, *Elementi di scienza politica*: "... within the lower classes another ruling class, or directing minority, necessarily forms, and often this new class is antagonistic to the class that holds possession of the legal government." Mosca also recognizes, besides this form of circulation which consists in the struggle between elites and the replacement of an old elite by a new one, that other form which consists in the renewal of the existing elite by the accession of individuals from the lower classes of society; and he examines in a number of different contexts the relative ease or difficulty of access to the elite. He is led from this to distinguish between mobile and immobile societies, according to the degree of openness of the elite, and in contrast with Pareto he notices, and indeed exaggerates, as a significant characteristic of modern democratic societies the considerable volume of movement between the different social levels. In the modern European societies "... the ranks of the ruling classes have been held open. The barriers that kept individuals of the lower classes from entering the higher have been either removed or lowered, and the development of the old absolutist state into the modern representative state has made it possible for almost all political forces, almost all social values, to participate in the management of society" (*The Ruling Class*, p. 474).

The most prominent feature in Mosca's treatment of the circulation of elites is to be seen, however, in the kind of explanation which he seeks. He refers occasionally to the intellectual and moral qualities of the members of the elite, but, unlike Pareto, he does not attach supreme importance to these psychological characteristics. In the first place, he observes that such individual characteristics are frequently produced by social circumstances: "Courage in battle, impetuousness in attack, endurance in resistance—such are the qualities that have long and often been vaunted as a monopoly of the higher classes. Certainly there may be vast natural and—if we may say so—innate differences between one individual and another in these respects; but more than anything else traditions and environmental influences are the things that keep them high, low or just average, in any large group of human beings" (ibid., p. 64). Secondly, he makes scarcely any reference to such individual characteristics in his explanation of the rise and fall of elites; he explains these phenomena by the germination of new interests and ideals in a society, as well as by the appearance of new problems: "What we see is that as soon as there is a shift in the balance of political forces—when, that is, a need is felt that capacities different from the old should assert themselves in the management of the state, when the old capacities, therefore, lose some of their importance or changes in their distribution occur—then the manner in which the ruling class is constituted changes also. If a new source of wealth develops in a society, if the practical importance of knowledge grows, if an old religion declines or a new one is born, if a new current of ideas spreads, then, simultaneously, far-reaching dislocations occur in the ruling class" (ibid., p. 65). As Meisel has noted[5] this line of argument brings Mosca close to Marxist ideas, and since he is aware of this danger he tries strenuously to distinguish his theory from that of Marx by insisting upon the limitations of the economic interpretation of history and by emphasizing the influence of moral and religious ideas in social change. Mosca's position on this question is, in fact, not very different from that of Max Weber, in rejecting an exclusive and one-sided economic interpretation of history; but he is less willing than Weber was to acknowledge the influence of Marx's thought because of his pronounced hostility to the labour movement and to socialism.

Two other writers have discussed, quite independently, the problem of the circulation of elites, and we may briefly consider their views at this stage. The Belgian historian, Henri Pirenne, in an essay on "Les périodes de l'histoire sociale du capitalisme,"[6] advanced the hypothesis that each distinct period in the development of capitalism[7] was characterized by the dominance of a different class of capitalists. "With every change in economic development, there is a break in continuity. The capitalists who have been active up to that point recognize, one may say, that they are incapable of adapting themselves to the circumstances produced by hitherto unknown needs, which require new means for their satisfaction. They retire from the struggle, and become an aristocracy whose members, if they participate at all in the management of affairs, participate only in a passive way by providing capital. In their place new men arise, bold and enterprising individuals who sail audaciously before the winds of change ...". Pirenne distinguishes four main periods in which such transformations have occurred—the rise of the town merchants from the eleventh century, the development of international trade in the thirteenth century, the emergence of new industries and of manufacturing towns in the sixteenth century, and finally the industrial revolution of the eighteenth century—and seeks to show that at each of these turning points new men rose from the lower strata of society to become the leaders of economic activity.

Some similar observations are made by Schumpeter in an essay on "Social classes in an ethnically homogeneous milieu."[8] Schumpeter distinguishes very clearly between different types of circulation, in sections of his essay which deal with "the rise and fall of families within a class," "movement across class lines" and "the rise and fall of whole classes." One of the most valuable features of Schumpeter's study is that it considers together the individual and the social factors in the circulation of elites. In the movement of families between classes, he argues, social ascent is influenced—leaving aside the operation of chance—by individual endowment in energy and intelligence, but also by social circumstances such as the openness of the upper class, and the opportunities for enterprise in new fields of activity. Similarly, in the rise and fall of whole classes, some weight must be attributed to the qualities of individuals, but a more important influence is exerted by structural changes affecting the functions of the elite groups. ". . . the position of each class in the total national structure depends, on the one hand, on the significance that is attributed to (its) function, and, on the other hand, on the degree to which the class successfully performs the function." Schumpeter illustrates this process by an examination of the rise of a warrior nobility in Germany, and its subsequent decline from the end of the fourteenth century as a result of the development of a national administrative system, and of the patrimonialization of landed property. The underlying causes of this decline are to be found in the loss in social importance of the function of individual combat—the demilitarization of society—and in the economic changes which favoured large landed estates.

The foregoing studies were all intended to contribute in

some way to the understanding of political change, either by accounting for changes in the personnel of the formal institutions of government, or in a broader sense, by explaining the fluctuations in the power or influence of particular groups in society. How far were they successful in formulating the main problems and in producing evidence to support their conclusions? There are far-reaching differences between Pareto's approach and that which was adopted by Mosca, Pirenne or Schumpeter. Pareto devotes most attention to the circulation of individuals between the elite and the non-elite; and this pre-occupation follows directly from his choice of "social equilibrium" as the main subject of his investigation. Like the modern functionalists—whose chief ancestor he is in an ideological as well as a scientific sense—Pareto sets out to study those factors which maintain a particular society, or a particular form of society, in existence; and, like them again, he tacitly excludes from his field of research any inquiry into the major differences between types of society or into the causes of change from one type of society to another. In Pareto's historical picture there are no real transformations of social structure but only an endless cyclical movement in which a declining elite is restored to vitality by the recruitment of new elements from the lower strata of the population, or is overthrown and replaced by a new elite which has been formed by these same elements in conditions where they are denied access, as individuals, to the established elite. Through all these movements the form of society remains unchanged, since it is defined abstractly as the rule of an elite over the majority of the population. There can be no sense in asking, from the standpoint which Pareto takes, whether there have been historical changes in the composition and cultural outlook of the elite, or in the relations between the elite and the masses. Whenever Pareto touches upon problems such as these, he at once recoils, and reaffirms that the main theme of his study is the general, abstract, and a historical question of the conditions of social equilibrium.

Mosca, Pirenne and Schumpeter, on the contrary, although they differ on many points, agree in recognizing that new social groups may be formed in a society as a result of economic or cultural changes, that such groups may then increase their social influence in so far as the kinds of activity in which they engage become of vital importance to society at large, and that these activities may in due course produce changes in the political system, and in the social structure as a whole. Their concern with the rise and fall of social groups, and particularly of those groups which are distinguished by their economic functions, shows the influence of Marx's theory of classes; and the same influence is apparent in the fact that they apply the term "class" rather than "elite" to such groups, and so present a model of society in which the complexity and historical variability of class structure figures more prominently than does the universal and unchanging division between a ruling elite and the masses. It is only in Mosca's work that the latter distinction finds a place at all, and, as I showed earlier, it is largely abandoned when he comes to discuss the political systems of modern societies. This is not to say that any of these writers wholly neglects the circulation of individuals between the elite groups (or upper class) and the lower strata of society, in his concern with the movement of social groups. Schumpeter, as we have seen, makes a very careful distinction between these different types of circulation, and so, in a less clear-cut fashion, does Mosca; only Pirenne, in this particular study, confines his attention to the formation of new classes. But on this point, too, they differ markedly from Pareto, since (as Schumpeter's work makes especially clear) they explain the circulation of individuals and families within the class system very largely by characteristics of the class structure itself, rather than by individual differences of ability and character.

The most distinctive feature of this conception of the circulation of elites—and this follows from the points I have already mentioned—is that it takes account of a real historical development, at least within the area of Western civilization, in the nature of elites, and of their relations with the rest of society, and accepts that the changes in technology, and in general culture, have produced different forms of class structure and of political power.

But although we can find, in the works of Mosca, Pirenne and Schumpeter, a more coherent account and more plausible explanations of the circulation of elites than is to be discovered in the writings of Pareto, these studies are still inadequate in many respects. One of their most obvious deficiencies is the lack of a proper method of investigation. Not one of these studies makes it possible to establish that there is, or is not, a constant connexion between the amount of circulation of individuals and groups in society and the extent of changes in the economic, political and cultural system: first, because they present no systematic comparisons between societies, and secondly, because they provide no exact measurement of the phenomena with which they deal. Pareto, Mosca, Kolabinska, Pirenne and Schumpeter all succeed in showing that some individuals change their class position, or move between the elite and the non-elite. They do this, in the main, by giving examples of individuals who have risen in the social hierarchy. But this does not tell us what we need most to know: namely, what *proportion* of the elite or upper class is recruited from the lower strata of society, and what proportion of those in the lower strata is enabled to rise. The outcome of this method of historical illustration seems very often to be an inflation of the amount of circulation in a society. William Miller, for example, has noted that historians, dealing with one aspect of elite recruitment during a recent period of American history, have greatly exaggerated the proportion of business leaders who have risen from the lower strata of society. "Virtually all the generalizations that go to make up this model (of recruitment to the business elite) are based upon a few remarkable life histories from the 'robber baron' period; ... Yet to read the lives of business leaders ... is to look almost in vain for working class or foreign origins, and even poor and unschooled farm boys are not conspicuous among such leaders."[9] It is clear that exact measurement of the circulation of individuals between the elite and the non-elite (which forms part of the study of what modern sociologists call "social mobility") presents great difficulties, even when it is attempted in present-day societies. Some of these difficulties have been indicated in a recent attempt to study social mobility on a comparative basis:[10] leaving aside a host of general problems of measurement, there are particular difficulties which arise from variations in the size of elites between one society and another, and from differences in the class structure of societies, which have quite different proportions of their population in agricultural or industrial work, and in manual or non-manual occupations.

One conclusion which emerges from considering these problems is that a simple distinction between the elite and the non-elite, such as Pareto used, is quite inadequate, for no calculation of the rate of movement into the elite from other sections of the population is likely to be meaningful unless we know something about the size and structure of the elite, and about the general class structure, in a particular society. However, in the study of the circulation of elites in present-day societies it is at least possible to collect the necessary data, through national sample surveys or through more intensive studies of particular elite groups. When we turn to historical studies of elite circulation the collection of data is itself a further difficulty, which was not seriously confronted by the earlier writers. The present lack of information is no doubt due, in part, to the fact that general historians have not usually been interested in this kind of quantitative investigation, and that social history, which would concern itself with these problems, has still to be developed. As William Miller observes in the essay which I quoted earlier: "One might have supposed that historians, largely occupied as they have been with the activities of ruling classes, would have been among the first to study systematically the problems of the recruitment and tenure of elites. This problem is an especially interesting one in a country such as the United States which has had no official caste systems and no legally established hereditary hierarchies. Yet most American historians have shied away from it."[11] The studies of the business elite in the volume which Miller has edited, a recent study of the Chinese *literati*,[12] and several studies of the political elite in various countries,[13] indicate that the necessary historical information can in some cases be discovered; but it may well be that, for many countries and periods, it will remain impossible to determine in any exact way how much movement there has been into and out of the elite.

Even if reasonably exact information about the circulation of elites in a large number of societies were made available, it would still be necessary, in order to demonstrate a connexion between this circulation and other social phenomena, to take a step which none of the earlier writers on elites attempted; namely, to undertake comprehensive and systematic comparisons between societies. Pareto suggests that the circulation of individuals between the elite and the non-elite is a constant and regular phenomenon. But is this so? Are there not substantial differences between societies in the rate of circulation? And if this is so, what are the causes of these differences and what are their effects in the political sphere? Mosca and others suggest that the rate of circulation is very high in modern societies, and that, in Mosca's words, "the modern representative state has made it possible for almost all political forces, almost all social values, to participate in the management of society." The investigations which I have just discussed do not confirm this view, but the modern industrial societies may still be a good deal more mobile than most other types of society. Another question which we may put concerns the relation between individual mobility and the rise and fall of elites or classes. Is it true, as Pareto argues, that revolutions occur when the rate of circulation of individuals is too low? These questions indicate an array of problems which can certainly not be solved on the basis of present knowledge, and which the early writers only posed, although they expressed themselves in what purported to be explanatory statements.

Pareto, as we have seen, focused his attention upon this movement of individuals in the circulation of elites. The other writers, who dealt at greater length with the movement of groups—the rise and fall of elites—do not seem to me to have advanced very far beyond what Marx had already accomplished in accounting for the origins and development of social classes. In fact, they all attribute prime importance to the emergence of new interests in society. Mosca's "social forces" are very like Marx's "class interests," Pirenne deals entirely with the rise of new groups of capitalists, and Schumpeter explains the decline of an armed nobility very largely in economic terms. Where they diverge from Marxism is in dealing much more thoroughly with the development of sub-groups within the major social classes— new occupational groups, for instance—and, of course, in refraining from any discussion of the potential classless society which Marx discerned within modern capitalism.

Mosca, although he insists so strongly upon the influence of cultural and religious factors in the creation of new "social forces," does not produce or examine closely any historical instances which might bear out his claim that factors of this kind are sometimes of crucial importance in bringing about changes in the social structure. Schumpeter, in a later work —*Capitalism, Socialism and Democracy*—discusses the changes in culture which are helping to bring about the decline of capitalism, but he treats these changes as secondary and largely dependent upon changes in the economic order.

There is one question, in particular, which these writers fail to examine with even such close attention as Marx himself; namely, the nature and causes of revolutionary changes in society. This problem needs to be set out in broader terms than those which Marx—in his preoccupation with the nineteenth-century revolutions—employed. In the rise and fall of social groups two processes may be observed: one in which there is a gradual acquisition of the positions of power by individuals belonging to a new social stratum, sometimes through alliances with members of the established political elite; and another in which there is a violent confrontation between a rising social group and the established rulers of society. One of the objects of political studies is to discover, so far as possible, the conditions and causes of these different types of circulation of social groups. Pareto hardly touches upon the problem, and his observations upon revolutions are sparse and disconnected. Mosca, on the other hand, devotes a chapter of *The Ruling Class* to the subject of revolution, but it is one of the most disappointing sections of his work, providing little more than a descriptive account of a few revolutionary periods. It cannot be said that the work of other sociologists, after Marx, has added much to the explanation of revolutionary changes, in spite of the abundance of material supplied by our own revolutionary century. The most comprehensive and systematic discussion of these problems in recent years, is undoubtedly that by C. Brinton in his book *The Anatomy of Revolution*.[14] Brinton distinguishes as conditions which favour revolutionary change: economic progress in a society, bitter class antagonisms, desertion of the ruling class by the intellectuals, inefficient governmental machinery and a politically inept ruling class. The conditions do not differ widely from those which Marx proposed at various times, especially in his early writings, except that the formation of the revolutionary class itself receives much less attention; but they are set out as a framework for a much more rigorous comparative study. The usefulness of this conceptual framework may be seen by applying it to the revolutions of the twentieth century, most of which have occurred in industrially backward countries, which possessed in a high degree the characteristics which Brinton distinguishes: extreme class antagonisms produced by the immense differences between the rich and the poor, the defection of Westernized intellectuals, frequently influenced by Marxism, and the ineptitude of traditional ruling groups in dealing with economic problems and with the impact of more advanced societies.

One thing that emerges clearly from these later writings on the subject, and which confirms Marx's theory, is that modern revolutions cannot be explained by the activities of small elite groups—they are brought about by the actions of whole classes. These classes have to be led; but the elite group of leaders arises from, and to some extent along with, the formation and development of the class—it does not create the class, nor does it by itself bring about a revolutionary movement. The same is true, I think, in the case of more gradual changes in the position of groups in the hierarchy of power. It is because the situation of relatively large groups in the population changes that new elites can be formed and can, over a period of time, wrest a share in political power from the established rulers of society.

In studying the circulation of groups, as in studying the circulation of individuals, we have to confront many difficulties in the collection of data. The two studies overlap to some extent, and present the same problems, for it may be necessary to trace the movement of individuals in order to throw light upon the formation of new social groups or the decline of old ones. In most cases, however, it is somewhat easier to discover evidence for the rise and fall of social groups, because their existence and activities are likely to be documented in legal texts or in contemporary chronicles, or they may be inferred from a knowledge of other social institutions, such as systems of land tenure, and religious or military organization. But whichever aspect of the circulation of elites attracts our attention we can supplement historical knowledge of the phenomenon (and such knowledge could itself be greatly extended) by studies of the social movements of the twentieth century—studies which were beyond the powers of the earlier writers on elites. During the last two decades the circulation of elites in the industrial societies has been the object of numerous investigations, and the same attention is now being given to it in the under-developed countries. A review of the accumulated evidence from several societies of each type, which I shall undertake in the following two chapters, may enable us to formulate some more adequately supported generalizations than those which have been criticized here.

## NOTES

[1] *The Mind and Society*, III, p. 1430. The idea is stated in almost identical terms in his earlier book, *Les systèmes socialistes*, pp. 28–30.

[2] According to Pareto the principal spheres of logical action are the economic (or business) and the scientific. He exaggerates the rationality of behaviour

in these spheres, especially in the first, and underrates the degree of rationality in other forms of social action, e.g. in politics.

3 The concept of "residues" has been criticized at length by Morris Ginsberg, in an essay on "The Sociology of Pareto" which makes very plain the vagueness and inadequacy of Pareto's ideas on this subject. See his *Reason and Unreason in Society*.

4 Cf. Kolabinska, op. cit., p. 9, "In general, the elites which receive elements from outside themselves are in a better position to endure than those which exclude such elements."

5 See above, pp. 26–7.

6 *Bulletin de l'Académie royale de Belgique*, mai, 1914. An English version, which omitted many of the footnotes, was published in the *American Historical Review*, April, 1914.

7 It does not affect our present discussion that Pirenne discovers the origins of this development in a very early period, namely the eleventh century.

8 Originally published in the *Archiv für Sozialwissenschaft und Sozialpolitik*, Vol. 57, 1927. The English translation is in Joseph A. Schumpeter, *Imperialism and Social Classes*.

9 William Miller, "American Historians and the Business Elite" in William Miller (ed.), *Men in Business*. This view is confirmed by a comparative study of the recruitment of elites, which concludes that no country among the fourteen for which data were available has any considerable movement from the manual strata of the population into the upper levels. See S. M. Miller, "Comparative Social Mobility", *Current Sociology*, IX (1), 1960.

10 S. M. Miller, op. cit.

11 op. cit., p. 309.

12 Robert M. Marsh, *The Mandarins: The Circulation of Elites in China, 1600–1900*.

13 See especially, W. L. Guttsman, *The British Political Elite*; and the study of French Deputies by Mattei Dogan, in Dwaine Marvick (ed.), *Political Decision-Makers*.

14 See also the essay by L. Gottschalk, "Causes of Revolution", *American Journal of Sociology*, L (1), 1944; and for a short review of the problems and literature Ralf Dahrendorf, "Über einige Probleme der soziologischen Theorie der Revolution", *European Journal of Sociology*, II (1), 1961.

# IV

# INTELLECTUALS, MANAGERS AND BUREAUCRATS

AMONG the social groups which have risen to prominence in the tremendous social and political changes of the twentieth century three elites—the intellectuals, the managers of industry and the high government officials—have often been singled out as the inheritors of the functions of earlier ruling classes and as vital agents in the creation of new forms of society. How important have they really been in initiating change? How far are they the products of other, more fundamental, changes in society, or representatives of more powerful interests? Let us be clear at the outset that the attribution of such great social influence to these elite groups derives in the first place from the acceptance of the general theory of elites, and springs directly from the critique of Marxism which that theory supplied. For according to the Marxist view the most significant fact of recent Western history is the rise of the working class as a new social force; while the accounts which are given of the rise of the intellectuals, or managers, or bureaucrats, all challenge that view, and attempt to show that the transformations of capitalism lead to a "classless" recruitment of elites (i.e. a more or less perfect circulation of individuals between the various levels of prestige and power), but at the same time maintain in existence the distinction between a ruling elite and the masses (i.e. do not lead towards a classless society). In examining the rise of these elites, therefore, we shall need to consider, first, how they are related to the major social classes, and what modifications they have brought about in the class system of the capitalist countries, and secondly, what is the nature of their influence in the collectivist societies of the Soviet type.

Of these three groups the intellectuals are the most difficult to define, and their social influence is the most difficult to determine. We may begin by distinguishing between "intellectuals" and "intelligentsia." The latter term was first used in Russia in the nineteenth century to refer to those who had received a university education which qualified them for professional occupations; subsequently, its denotation has been extended by many writers, to include all those who are engaged in non-manual occupations. In this sense it is equivalent to the "new middle classes," within which we may distinguish between higher and lower strata—the higher comprising those in professional occupations, and the lower those in the more routine clerical and administrative jobs. The intellectuals, on the other hand, are generally regarded as comprising the much smaller group of those who contribute directly to the creation, transmission and criticism of ideas; they include writers, artists, scientists, philosophers, religious thinkers, social theorists, political commentators. The boundaries of the group may be difficult to determine with precision, and its lower levels merge with middle class occupations such as teaching and journalism, but its characteristic feature—direct concern with the culture of a society—is sufficiently clear.

Intellectuals are to be found in almost all societies—in non-literate societies as magicians and priests, as poets and minstrels, as genealogists, and so on, and in literate societies as philosophers, poets, dramatists, officials or lawyers—but their functions and their social importance vary considerably. In some societies the intellectuals have come close to being a governing elite. In China the *literati* formed, over long periods, a ruling stratum of this kind, which according to Max Weber grew out of an education for genteel *laymen*.[1] It was not a hereditary or exclusive group, since entry to it was by public competitive examination; but in practice it was largely recruited, during the feudal period, from important feudal families, and later on, from the higher social strata (including a high proportion of officials' families). Nevertheless, a careful statistical analysis of the *literati* in the period 1600–1900 indicates that some 30 per cent were recruited from the families of commoners; i.e. from a social level below the elite, although some of them certainly came from wealthy families.[2] In India, a similar situation existed, in the sense that the Brahmins constituted themselves a ruling stratum in the society; but there are important differences from the case of China, for the Brahmins were a hereditary caste, and their training was religious rather than literary. On the other hand, the clerics occupied a less dominant position in the European feudal societies, and only with the breakdown of feudalism did the intellectuals begin to assume a more important social role.

The origins of the modern intellectuals have generally been placed in the universities of medieval Europe.[3] The growth of the universities, associated with the spread of humanistic learning, made possible the formation of an intellectual class which was not a priestly caste, whose members were recruited from diverse social milieux, and which was in some measure detached from the ruling classes and ruling doctrines of feudal society. This intellectual class produced the thinkers of the Enlightenment, and in France particularly, the intellectuals established themselves as critics of society by their opposition to the ruling class and to the Church of the *ancien régime*. It is in this role, as critics of society, that the modern intellectuals have usually been considered. Their part in revolutionary movements, in the labour movement as a whole, and more recently in the transformation of the underdeveloped countries, has been emphasized in numerous writings, very often in the context of a critique of Marx's theory of the proletarian revolution. One of the earliest writers to present such an account of the influence of intellectuals was a Polish revolutionary, Waclaw Machajski, who set out in a number of books, and especially in *The Intellectual Worker* (1905),[4] the theory that the socialist movement actually expressed the ideology of dissatisfied intellectuals, and that its success would result, not in a classless society, but in the creation of a new ruling class of intellectuals, allied with the new middle class, in a type of society which he called "State capitalism." Machajski himself was not entirely pessimistic about the future of socialism, and he considered that through the general improvement of education the predominance of the intellectuals might be diminished and a classless society eventually attained. But his work as a whole received little attention and the idea of the revolutionary intellectuals was taken up in the main by opponents of socialism; originally by Max Nomad, and later by H. D. Lasswell, who propounded the view which is now so widely held that most of the revolutions of the twentieth century have been led by intellectuals who succeeded in establishing themselves in power under the banner of socialism.

The role of the intellectuals has been very differently conceived by some other writers. We saw earlier that Mosca regarded the intellectuals as a more or less independent group standing between the bourgeoisie and the proletariat, which might form the nucleus of a new and more worthy elite. In the final pages of his *Teorica dei governi e governo parlamentare* he expresses his hopes thus: "If there is any social class prepared to set aside, if only for a while, the private interest, and able to perceive the common good with the detachment needed, it is certainly the one which, thanks to its exacting intellectual training, has what should make for nobility of character, for broad horizons and for enlarged faculties ... that class, and that class alone, will freely sacrifice a present good in order to avert a future evil." A very similar conception was outlined several decades later by Karl Mannheim, who discerned in the "socially unattached intelligentsia" a relatively classless stratum, recruited from an increasingly inclusive area of social life, bound together by education, and subsuming in itself all those interests with which social life is permeated.[5] Because of these characteristics the intellectuals are capable, according to Mannheim, of acquiring a relatively complete and objective view of their society, and especially of the different interest groups within it, and of acting independently to promote more general social interests.

There is some truth in both the accounts which we have considered. Intellectuals have taken a prominent part in radical and revolutionary movements, and they still do so, as the events of Poland and Hungary in 1956, the revolution in Cuba, and anti-colonial movements in many countries bear witness. But the attraction of intellectuals towards the socialist movement is explicable in other ways than by the theory that they form a new elite which is struggling for power under the deceptive slogans of socialism and the classless society. The labour movement in Western societies was not a simple protest movement. Unlike the sporadic revolts of slaves or peasants who could express their aspirations in the religious imagery which they found ready to hand, it involved, almost from the beginning, a theory of society, in the elaboration of which intellectuals necessarily had an important role. They were attracted to the socialist movement because they found there a place of honour, and also, in some degree, an ideal of social organization which had some of the characteristics—rationality, impartiality and even other-worldliness—which are vital to intellectual life itself. Another factor which was equally important, and perhaps more important, was the social origins of the intellectuals. In many modern societies the universities, and intellectual occupations in general, have constituted the principal means by which talented individuals from the lower strata of society could rise to more important positions. As a result the social composition of the intellectual elite has usually differed considerably from that of other elites, and it has always been likely that many intellectuals would ally themselves with the working-class movement.

This view suggests that the intellectual elite, rather than having its own occupational interests, will be associated with, or divided in its allegiance between, major social classes. The second view, according to which the intellectuals form a group which is capable of taking an objective view of society and of defending consistently some general interest of society as a whole, sets the intellectual elite above classes altogether while still denying that intellectuals are likely to develop a specific group interest of their own.

Neither of these accounts does justice to the diversity and mutability of the situation of intellectuals in modern societies. In the first place, there are important national differences among the industrial countries of Europe and North America. Raymond Aron has observed, in *The Opium of the Intellectuals*, that French intellectuals have higher social prestige, are less closely associated with the administrative and practical aspects of political life, and are more radical critics of their society, than are the intellectuals of Britain, Germany or the USA. A study of members of the French Chamber of Deputies from 1871 to 1958 shows that more than half of the 6,000 deputies elected during that period were intellectuals in a broad sense—writers, university teachers, lawyers, journalists, scientists, engineers, schoolteachers—and concludes that: "In France, at least, it was the intellectuals who most impassioned political debates in the Assembly under the Fourth Republic, as under the Third. They were very often the most intransigent ideologues. Their 'minds were similarly furnished' in the sense that they were apt to pose problems abstractly, with more or less sincerity, and often to expound them with ability. But this aptitude meant that they often proposed unrealistic solutions; and that they fixed upon subtleties and neglected essentials, thus uselessly complicating and prolonging parliamentary debates by inventing false problems and disagreeing among themselves."[6] It is interesting to observe, also, from a study of the great men of France, as recorded in the *Petit Larousse*, how prominently intellectuals in the most exclusive sense—writers, artists and scholars—figure in the list, and thus how great their social prestige is considered to be; over several centuries they form by far the largest group, accounting for nearly half the total, and their pre-eminence steadily increased up to the end of the nineteenth century (the latest period covered by the study).[7] In Britain, intellectuals have not possessed such great social prestige as in France, nor have they been so prominent in political life, either by membership of parliament, or by any collective activity of social thought and criticism. Only on rare occasions have groups of intellectuals attracted any great public attention, or seemed to have a direct political influence: among the more obvious instances over the past century and a half are the Utilitarian philosophers, the Christian socialists, the early Fabians, and the intellectuals who were associated with the Left Book Club and the anti-Fascist organizations of the 1930s.

A second important characteristic is that the intellectual elite, in most countries and at most times, is one of the least homogeneous or cohesive of elites, and displays a considerable variety of opinion on cultural and political questions. By no means all intellectuals belong or have belonged politically to the left, and at the present time, for instance, it is probably the case that most intellectuals in the West European countries and in the USA belong to the right. There is much evidence that the political attitudes of intellectuals are influenced very strongly by their social class origins; for example, there was a striking difference in France between the students of the former *Ecole libre des Sciences politiques*, recruited almost entirely from the upper class and strongly right wing in their attitudes, and the students of the *Ecole Normale*, recruited much more widely from the middle class, working class and peasantry, and predominantly left wing in their attitudes. What is not at all clear is whether intellectuals are *less* influenced than are other elites by their social class origins, because of the nature of their activities and way of life. Again, there are important historical fluctuations in the social attitudes of intellectuals, which are brought about by more general changes in society. In the 1930s a majority of the European intellectuals, and many in the USA, were supporters of the political left; but since the early 1950s there has been a pronounced movement towards the right, which may be accounted for by changes in social conditions, under the influence of welfare legislation, or by changes in the character of the intellectual elite itself.

In this context, two features of the recent history of intellectuals in the industrial societies need to be considered. The size and the internal differentiation of the intellectual elite have both increased, especially at the lower levels, with the expansion of university education and the growth of scientific, technical and professional occupations. At the same time, changes have occurred in the relative importance of different groups within the intellectual elite; experts of one kind or another have come to predominate over the more literary and philosophical exponents of general cultural or social ideas. The growing social importance of natural scientists is clearly to be seen in the amount of public attention which their activities and needs attract, and in the pressures which are developing to give scientists a larger part in the shaping of public policy, through membership of advisory bodies and increased representation in government and administration (for example, by the creation of a Ministry of Science). It may be as a consequence of these developments that intellectuals have tended to become less radical critics of society as a whole and to be more concerned with solving the kind of short-term, specific problem which arises out of the complex activities of the industrial societies in which they live. In this sense, the influence of intellectuals has increased in one of the directions which Mosca expected; but the very fact that they are increasingly engaged in such circumscribed, expert tasks, makes them less qualified for the position of a ruling elite, because they lack any distinctive group organization or ideology. It is in the underdeveloped countries at the present time that intellectuals most often form a cohesive and radical elite which plays a significant part in political life.

A second group which has attracted attention as a potential ruling elite is that constituted by the managers of industry. For a time, the rise of the managers in modern society became a focal point of sociological controversy, largely under the influence of James Burnham's theory of the managerial revolution.[8] The basic idea of this theory was stated much earlier by Veblen in *The Engineers and the Price System*. Veblen argued that capitalism, i.e. a system of production directed mainly by the owners of the means of production, could not last, because of its inefficient use of industrial resources, but he did not accept the Marxist view that its downfall would be brought about by the working class, and that it would be followed by a classless society. He saw the principal opposition to capitalist industry in the technological specialists—the "engineers"—upon whose work the operation of modern industry depends, and who are in a position, as he claims, to make the next move. "They are, by force of circumstance, the keepers of the community's material welfare; although they have hitherto been acting, in effect, as keepers and providers of free income for the kept classes. They are thrown into the position of responsible directors of the industrial system, and by the same move they are in a position to become arbiters of the community's material welfare. They are becoming class-conscious, and they are no longer driven by a commercial interest, in any such degree as will make them a vested interest in that commercial sense in which the syndicated owners and the federated workmen are vested interests. They are, at the same time, numerically and by habitual outlook, no such heterogeneous and unwieldy body as the federated workmen, whose numbers and scattering interest has left all their endeavours substantially nugatory" (op. cit., p. 74).

Burnham's thesis is essentially similar, but it is set out in a more elaborate form. He argues that we are living in a period of transition from one type of society to another, from capitalist society (i.e. a society characterized by a particular mode of production, by the dominance of industrialists and bankers, and by specific systems of belief or ideologies) to a type of society which he proposes to call the "managerial society." Before explaining the process of transition to this society—the "managerial revolution"—he discusses the principal alternative theory of the decline of capitalism, the Marxist theory of proletarian revolution. His criticism is along familiar lines: first, that the Russian revolution did not inaugurate a socialist society, and secondly, that in most of the advanced industrial countries there have been no proletarian revolutions, and in the few cases where they occurred they were unsuccessful (e.g. Germany in 1918). His own theory involves first of all a statement of who are the managers, and then a demonstration that the group which he has defined is in fact becoming a ruling elite in society. Burnham distinguishes two principal sections among the managers: the scientists and technologists, and the directors and co-ordinators of the process of production. The latter are the managers *par excellence*, and Burnham distinguishes them from the "engineers" in Veblen's sense, even though many of them may have scientific or technical qualifications. They are, in fact, the top executives or company directors of business corporations, and Burnham's analysis of their position in society depends in large measure upon establishing that there has developed in modern industrial societies a radical separation between the ownership and the control of industry. The idea of such a separation was familiar to nineteenth-century students of society (including Marx) who observed the consequences of the development of joint stock companies; but its significance has increased with the appearance of the modern giant corporation, which was first systematically examined by A. A. Berle and G. C. Means in their book *The Modern Corporation and Private Property*. Burnham's argument is that the managers are taking over the economic power which was formerly in the hands of the capitalist owners of industry, and are thus acquiring the power to shape the whole social system. He supports his thesis—which requires not only that the managers shall be a distinct social group, but that they shall be a cohesive group, aware of their group interests in a struggle for power—by attempting to show that the individualistic ideology of capitalism is being replaced by a managerialist ideology. As evidence for the latter point he presents the experiences of the Fascist corporate state in Germany and Italy (which has not survived), of the Soviet Union (which is not most satisfactorily interpreted as a managerial society, as I shall try to show later in this chapter), and of the limited amount of state planning in the USA and other Western countries.

Subsequent criticism has made it clear that the fundamental notion of the separation of ownership and control in modern industrial societies is at best a half truth. There is a close connexion between the owners and the managers of industry in several respects. In the first place, the managers are very often owners, in the sense that they have substantial shareholdings in their companies; and although shareholding may be quite widely dispersed this only makes it easier for a small number of large shareholders to control the policies of the company.[9] Secondly, even when managers are not important shareholders in their own companies, they are usually wealthy men; as C. Wright Mills points out in *The Power Elite*, "the chief executives and the very rich are *not* two distinct and clearly segregated groups. They are both very much mixed up in the corporate world of property and privilege ..." (p. 119). Thirdly, the recruitment of managers is predominantly from the upper strata of society. In the USA, according to Mills, "the top executives of 1950 are not country boys who have made good in the city," nor are they immigrants or even sons of immigrants; "these urban, white, Protestant Americans were born into families of the upper and upper middle classes. Their fathers were mainly entrepreneurs: 57 per cent are sons of business men; 14 per cent of professional men; 15 per cent of farmers." This conclusion is confirmed by several other studies. William Miller has shown, in a careful investigation of the social origins of 190 prominent American business leaders in the first decade of the present century, that already at that time the notion that the typical successful business man had risen from the lowest strata of society was obsolete.[10] Less than 10 per cent of those he studied were born abroad, and only 1 per cent could be regarded as "poor immigrants." Most of them came from old-established American families, in the larger towns and cities; and 80 per cent of them were from business or professional families. A very thorough study of the upper class and the business elite in Philadelphia in 1940 concludes that ". . . the upper class contributed considerably more than its share of leaders within the business community: 75 per cent of the bankers, 51 per cent of the lawyers, 45 per cent of the engineers, and 42 per cent of the business men listed in *Who's Who* were also members of the upper class (i.e. belonged to families listed in the *Social Register*). In addition, of the 532 directorships in industrial and financial institutions reported by members of the elite, 60 per cent were reported by members of the upper class. Finally, the leading bankers and lawyers in the city were members of the upper class. The presidents, and over 80 per cent of the directors in the six largest banks were Proper Philadelphians, as were the senior partners in the largest law firms.[11]

In Britain a survey of directors of large public companies has shown that between 50 and 60 per cent began their careers with the advantage of having business connexions in the family, while another 40 per cent came from families of landowners, professional men and others of similar social level.[12]

It is evident, then, that the top managers and the owners of property are so intimately connected as to form, in the main, a single social group. The case of the middle and lower levels of management is scarcely different, for the social area of recruitment is not very much wider, and since most of the managers at these levels are aiming to reach the higher executive positions they have, for the most part, the same social attitudes and they seek to establish the same connexions as those at the top. As they mount the management ladder so they acquire more substantial property interests. In all this there is little to suggest an imminent "managerial revolution," or to give verisimilitude to Burnham's sketch of the new managerial ideology. The managers, especially the top managers, form an important functional group in industrial societies; they are an elite in the sense that they have high prestige and take important economic decisions, and that they are increasingly aware of their position as a functional group (and this awareness is fostered by the development of systematic studies and training in management), but they are not independent of the upper class of property owners, and they are not becoming a new "ruling class."

We have now to consider a third social group—that of the high government officials—which appears to many observers as an increasingly powerful elite in modern societies. The concern of sociologists with the bureaucratic elite originated in the work of Max Weber, in the course of his long controversy "with the ghost of Karl Marx" and with Marx's followers. Weber's opposition to socialism was inspired by a fear that it would result in the loss of individual freedom and in the more or less total regimentation of social life. Where Marx saw in the history of modern societies a concentration of the means of production in the hands of a small capitalist class, whose dispossession by the working class would be the initial step to inaugurate a period of increasing human liberty, Weber saw a process of concentration of the means of administration which would reach its apogee in a socialist society, with the direst consequences for the individual. ". . . the development of the modern state is initiated through the action of the prince. He paves the way for the expropriation of the autonomous and 'private' bearers of executive power who stand beside him, of those who in their own right possess the means of administration, warfare and financial organization . . . The whole process is a complete parallel to the development of the capitalist enterprise through gradual expropriation of the independent producers. In the end, the modern state controls the total means of political organization. . . ."[13]

Weber did not believe that the power of bureaucracy could be checked by political authorities, even in a democratic system: "Under normal conditions the power position of a fully developed bureaucracy is always overwhelming. The 'political master' finds himself in the position of the 'dilettante' who stands opposite the 'expert,' facing the trained official who stands within the management of administration. This holds whether the 'master' whom the bureaucracy serves is a 'people,' equipped with the weapons of 'legislative initiative,' the 'referendum,' and the right to remove officials, or a parliament, elected on a more aristocratic or more democratic basis and equipped with the right to vote a lack of confidence. . . ."[14]

There can be no doubt that Weber's interpretation was unduly influenced by the example of the Prussian bureaucracy, and of the ineffectiveness of liberal politicians in Germany. Nevertheless, it has seemed to many observers that his thesis of the increasing power of bureaucracy has gained support from the events of recent European history; in particular, from the experiences of the socialist revolution in Russia, and from the consequences of the more extensive control of economic activity by the state in the democratic industrial countries. The application of Weber's ideas to the Soviet social system has been made most fully and explicitly by a Yugoslav critic of totalitarian communism, Milovan Djilas, in his book *The New Class*. Djilas refers to "This new class, the bureaucracy, or more accurately the political bureaucracy," which, he says, has all the characteristics of earlier ruling classes as well as some new characteristics of its own. The new class is "made up of those who have special privileges and economic preference because of the administrative monopoly they hold." But Djilas has to admit that its members are not government officials or administrators in the ordinary sense: ". . . a more detailed analysis will show that only a special stratum of bureaucrats, those who are not administrative officials, make up the core of the governing bureaucracy [or new class]. This is actually a party or political bureaucracy. Other officials are only the apparatus under the control of the new class." Eventually he has to concede that "the party makes the class," but he attempts to avoid the consequences of this statement by saying that the class then "grows as a result and uses the party as a basis. The class grows stronger, while the party grows weaker." Finally, he attempts to bring the phenomenon within the scope of Marxist theory by asserting that the new class is defined by its ownership of the means of production: ". . . the proof that it is a special class lies in its ownership and its special relations to other classes . . . The Communist political bureaucracy uses, enjoys, and disposes of nationalized property."

In my view, this is a very misleading analysis of the elites in Soviet society. As Djilas himself admits, the new class is not a bureaucracy in the strict sense, because it is not made up of government officials and administrators; in fact, it is not a bureaucracy at all, since those who do compose it— the leading party members—are *not* bureaucrats, any more than the managers of industry are bureaucrats.[15] They are *political leaders* who rise to power in the party by the exercise of political abilities—tactical skill, cunning, persuasiveness, energy, perseverance and so on—not by passing examinations in Marxism–Leninism.[16] Similarly, the dominance which the party itself exercises is political, not bureaucratic. Djilas really admits this when he says that "the party makes the (new) class," but he tries to soften the force of the statement by adding that subsequently, "the class grows stronger, while the party grows weaker." There is no evidence at all that the Communist Party in any communist country has grown weaker in this particular way; what Djilas succeeds in expressing is a moral evaluation, an assertion of the decline of the ideal party, the revolutionary proletarian party. Lastly, it is a mistake to suppose that the party rules because it controls the means of production; on the contrary, it controls the means of production because it has political power. As a Polish sociologist has argued, ". . . the nineteenth century conception of social class, in both the liberal and the Marxian interpretations, has lost much of its applicability in the modern world. In situations where changes of social structure are to a greater or lesser degree governed by the decision of the political authorities, we are a long way from . . . classes conceived of as groups determined by their relations to the means of production or, as others would say, by their relations to the market . . . In situations where the political authorities can overtly and effectively change the class structure; where the privileges that are most essential for social status, including that of a higher share in the national income, are conferred by a decision of the political authorities; where a large part or even the majority of the population is included in a stratification of the type to be found in a bureaucratic hierarchy—the nineteenth-century concept of class becomes more or less an anachronism, and class conflicts give way to other forms of social antagonism."[17] This makes it clear that, while the lower levels of the social hierarchy may be bureaucratically organized, the ruling group itself is a political authority.

I do not wish to suggest that the high state officials are without influence in the USSR and other communist countries; only that they are not a ruling class. Even in the

Stalinist period, the ruling party had obviously to take some account of the attitudes and aspirations of the various elite groups, including the officials; and in the more liberal Krushchev regime it is plain that high officials, industrial managers, intellectuals and others, have some independent influence upon social policies, though this is still severely limited by the surveillance of the party.

Does the situation of officials in the Western democracies differ at all from the foregoing? Many writers have drawn attention to what they regard as the increasing power of bureaucracy, which they explain by the increase in the range of activities undertaken by the state, and by the growing complexity of public administration. A critic of the French administrative elite has described it in the following terms: "They [the high officials] constitute a supreme and sovereign self-recruiting body, immune from political intervention, a rock against which all political storms beat ineffectively and in vain . . ."[18]; while another writer, considering the progress of a "managerial revolution" in France, has observed that "two groups of experts are tending to assume a leading position in the state as in the economy. The elite of the administration is recruited essentially among the *Inspecteurs des finances* and the members of the *Conseil d'Etat*; it is a general staff which radiates everywhere. Since these administrators frequently transfer to the private sector, they are to be found in the banks and in large-scale industrial and commercial enterprises. The second source is the graduates of the *Ecole polytechnique*, who form the elite of the technical departments of state, but are also increasingly the managers of large scale industry."[19]

Such arguments have been most common in France, since the power of a bureaucracy stands out most clearly when the political authority itself is weak or unstable, but they are encountered in all the Western countries in one form or another. Sometimes, as in the work by André Siegfried quoted above, the argument is connected with the general thesis of the "managerial revolution," and it is suggested that the managers of private industry and of nationalized undertakings and the high government officials are together developing into a ruling elite. This idea is supported by the observation that there is a growing interchange of personnel between these different sectors of management and administration. I have shown earlier that the managers do not constitute an independent power elite, and a similar demonstration can be made in the case of officials. Their policy-making powers, however much they may have increased, are ultimately subject to the control of a political authority, and the conflict between political parties in the democratic countries is one of the means by which this control is made effective. Another means is what we may term the ethical code of the bureaucracy itself, and particularly the doctrine of political neutrality; in many Western countries, and notably in Britain, this doctrine exerts a restraining influence upon any ambition of high officials to usurp the policy-making powers of political leaders. Furthermore, in the case of officials, as in the case of industrial managers, it is evident from recent studies that they are closely associated with the upper classes of society; and in so far as they do directly influence public policy it is more likely to be along the lines of class interests than along the lines of their own particular aims as a rising elite of power. In Britain, a study by R. K. Kelsall has shown that, while the social area of recruitment to the administrative class of the higher civil service broadened between 1929 and 1950, there were still few recruits from the lower strata of the working class (semi-skilled and unskilled workers) which comprise some 30 per cent of the total population; and on the other hand, 30 per cent of the higher civil servants came from families of property owners and professional men which account for only 3 per cent of the population.[20] My own study of the French higher civil service indicates an even greater bias in recruitment: at the top level, in the *grands corps de l'Etat*, 84 per cent of the officials come from upper and upper middle class families, and less than 1 per cent come from the families of industrial workers or agricultural labourers.[21] Moreover, both in Britain and in France, the higher civil servants have for the most part been educated in independent, upper class schools and in socially exclusive institutions of higher education, and in this way the social opinions of the upper class have been perpetuated and reinforced. In France, the *Ecole libre des Sciences politiques* had a particularly important role, up to 1945, in the formation of an administrative elite within the upper class. Its founder, Emile Boutmy, expressed himself clearly on the subject: "Privilege has gone, democracy cannot be halted. The higher classes, as they call themselves, are obliged to acknowledge the right of the majority, and they can only maintain their political dominance by invoking the right of the most capable. Behind the crumbling ramparts of their prerogatives and of tradition the tide of democracy must encounter a second line of defence, constructed of manifest and useful abilities, of superior qualities whose prestige cannot be gainsaid . . ."[22] The postwar reforms of recruitment to the French higher civil service, including the establishment of the *Ecole Nationale d'Administration*, have changed the ethos of education for the administrative elite— have made it more "managerial" and less "upper class"— but they have not yet altered significantly the social area of recruitment. In the USA, on the other hand, the absence of a comprehensive career civil service, especially in the higher grades, has prevented the formation of an administrative elite, and has at the same time made it of less concern to upper-class families to place some of their members in the administration.[23] C. Wright Mills came to the view that the absence of a genuine bureaucracy was an important factor in allowing the creation of an irresponsible power elite in American society: "The United States has never and does not now have a genuine civil service, in the fundamental sense of a reliable civil service career, or of an independent bureaucracy effectively above political party pressure ... neither executives nor politicians really want a group of expert administrators who are genuinely independent of party considerations, and who, by training and experience, are the depository of the kind of skills needed to judge carefully the consequences of alternative policies."[24] But to argue in this way is to neglect all the experience of the European societies, in which the closest association has existed between the high officials of a genuine bureaucracy and the upper class in society.

This account of three elites which have attained prominence in modern societies suggests a number of interesting conclusions about the relations between elites and classes, and about the circulation of elites. Neither the intellectuals, nor the industrial managers, nor the bureaucrats can be seriously regarded as contenders for the place of the governing elite. None of these groups is sufficiently cohesive or sufficiently independent to be considered in such a light. The intellectuals are the most obviously divided among themselves, in normal circumstances, but all three groups show a lack of cohesion in the fact that they have not produced any doctrine which would express their specific importance and aims in society. A study of their characteristics brings to light a problem which was cogently stated by Carl J. Friedrich, in a criticism of the elite theories: "No attempt is made by Pareto to show that the 'elite,' as defined by him, possesses a distinct group character ...," and further, "... both writers (Mosca and Pareto) smuggle in as an unproven assumption or major premise what is the most problematical part of all elite doctrines, ... that those who play a role in government constitute a coherent group ..."[25] In spite of the many difficulties presented by the concept of class, I think it is a great deal easier to demonstrate the existence of broad class interests in modern democratic societies (with the evidence provided by the formation of specific organizations, by political ideologies and by voting behaviour) than to show that elite groups such as those we have examined have any similar collective interests, or even a collective "elite-consciousness."

The autonomy of these elites is limited, as we have seen, in various ways. They have class affiliations, which may be multiple as in the case of the intellectuals, or single, as is mainly the case with the managers and bureaucrats; and so they must be regarded as in some degree the representatives of social classes. The bureaucrats are controlled directly by political authorities, either by a single party as in the communist countries, or by several parties as in the democratic countries. The significance of the increasing influence of these elites seems to be not that each of them is a potential ruling class engaged in a struggle for supreme power, but that the competition and conflict among them may restrict the power of those who are the rulers of society at a given time.

## NOTES

[1] Max Weber, "The Chinese Literati", in H. H. Gerth and C. Wright Mills (eds.), *From Max Weber*.

[2] Robert M. Marsh, *The Mandarins: The Circulation of Elites in China, 1600–1900*.

[3] See Jacques Le Goff, *Les intellectuels au Moyen Age*, and Karl Mannheim, "The Problem of the Intelligentsia", in *Essays on the Sociology of Culture*.

[4] His books are in Russian and have not been translated. His ideas were first expounded in English by Max Nomad in *Rebels and Renegades*, from which I take this account.

[5] Karl Mannheim, *Ideology and Utopia*, p. 136 et seq.

[6] Mattei Dogan, "Political Ascent in a Class Society: French Deputies 1870–1958", in D. Marvick (ed.), *Political Decision-Makers*, p. 67.

[7] Alain Girard (ed.), *La réussite sociale en France*, pp. 239–40. As the editor

remarks, it would be interesting to obtain similar material from various countries in order to establish a basis for comparing the prestige and influence of intellectuals in different environments. Unfortunately, a beginning has still to be made, or even envisaged; the latest elaborate and bulky symposium on the intellectuals—*The Intellectuals: A Controversial Portrait*, edited by G. B. de Huszar—still relies largely upon impressionistic accounts of their social role.

8 James Burnham, *The Managerial Revolution*.

9 See P. Sargant Florence, *The Logic of British and American Industry*.

10 "American Historians and the Business Elite", in William Miller (ed.), *Men in Business*.

11 E. Digby Baltzell, *An American Business Aristocracy*, p. 431.

12 G. H. Copeman, *Leaders of British Industry: A Study of the Careers of More than a Thousand Public Company Directors*.

13 Max Weber, "Politics as a Vocation" in H. H. Gerth and C. Wright Mills, *From Max Weber*.

14 Max Weber, "Bureaucracy", ibid.

15 Cf. C. Wright Mills, *The Power Elite* (p. 133), "The bureaucratic career, properly defined, does not mean merely a climb up, from one level to the next, of a hierarchy of offices. It does involve that, but more importantly, it means the setting up of strict and unilateral qualifications for each office occupied. Usually these qualifications involve both specified formal training and qualifying examinations."

16 An American study of the Soviet bureaucracy, John A. Armstrong, *The Soviet Bureaucratic Elite: A Case Study of the Ukrainian Apparatus*, presents much the same thesis of rule by a bureaucracy. The author shows, in fact, that there has been an increasing emphasis upon the formal training of party officials in special party schools, but he does not show that ascent to the topmost positions of power is dependent upon success in this educational system, i.e. upon formal qualifications, rather than upon success in practical political leadership.

17 Stanislaw Ossowski, *Class Structure in the Social Consciousness*, p. 184.

18 H. Lüthy, *The State of France*, p.17.

19 André Siegfried, *De la IIIème a la IVème République*, p. 246.

20 R. K. Kelsall, *Higher Civil Servants in Britain*, p. 153.

21 This study is to be published under the title *Bureaucracy and Social Classes in France*.

22 Letter of 25th February 1871.

23 See R. Bendix, *Higher Civil Servants in American Society*. The recruitment is similar to that in Britain or France in so far as few higher civil servants come from working class families, but the social composition differs as a whole in being more predominantly middle class and lower middle class. Moreover, the American higher officials had a more diversified educational background, as well as being drawn from a variety of previous occupations.

24 C. Wright Mills, *The Power Elite*, pp. 239, 241.

25 Carl J. Friedrich, *The New Image of the Common Man*, pp. 257–8.

# V

## TRADITION AND MODERNITY: ELITES IN THE DEVELOPING COUNTRIES

THERE is no context in which the idea of elites is invoked more frequently at the present time than in discussions of the problems and prospects of the "underdeveloped countries." This should cause no surprise, for as we have seen already there is a profound association between changes in social structure and the rise and fall of elites. Economic, political, or other changes first bring about modifications in the prestige and power of different social groups, and those groups which are increasing their power then seek to take control of the changes and to press them forward. At the same time, the need for outstanding leaders and elites is most keenly felt by the population wherever complex and difficult social changes are taking place and the familiar ways of life are disappearing. In the present-day developing countries, therefore, we have an excellent opportunity to examine the social forces which are creating new elites, as well as the activities of the elites themselves in the attempted transformation of their societies into modern, economically advanced nations.

Each of these countries has, of course, some unique features and problems arising from its history, its geographical situation, or its particular relationships with other nations, which may have a greater or lesser influence upon its development; but there are also many important characteristics which are either common to all the underdeveloped countries, or are to be found in those belonging to a particular type. Leaving aside, for the present purpose, the factors of size and natural resources, we may distinguish four main categories of under-developed countries, within each of which there are important similarities of social structure and culture: (I) the African states; (II) the Arab states of the Middle East and North Africa; (III) the Asian states; and (IV) the Latin-American states. The countries belonging to the first group have established themselves by means of anti-colonial struggles which have affected profoundly their political regimes. They have to face, in addition to the problems of economic development, those of consolidating a national community formed out of tribal groups, whose existence within their frontiers is in some measure the result of the arbitrary division of Africa among the colonial powers. Among the countries of the second group, a number have been formed by independence struggles against direct colonial rule, but many others have enjoyed political independence for some time and have had chiefly to resist the indirect control of their economic resources by foreign powers. Their political problems are mainly those of breaking down feudal and autocratic systems of government, which are linked with highly inegalitarian and rigid class systems. The third group, that of the Asian countries, is characterized especially by the fact that these are, for the most part, countries of ancient civilization in which traditional social institutions are very strongly established. They also are countries which have liberated themselves very recently from colonial rule, and although they do not confront major problems of integrating tribal groups into a national community, as is the case with the African countries, they face some similar problems of national integration in so far as they are divided into castes or linguistic regions (as in India), or into ethnically and linguistically separate groups (e.g. Tamils and Sinhalese in

Ceylon, Malays and Chinese in Malaya). The fourth group, that of the Latin American countries, differs in important respects from all the others. These countries are, for the most part, more advanced economically, and they are already urban rather than agrarian societies,[1] although they have only recently begun to industrialize on a large scale; and they have been politically independent for a relatively long time. Thus, their political problems are not to the same extent those of national integration, although in some of them, such as Peru, the large Indian population has still to acquire full citizenship; nor has recent political activity been directly inspired by nationalism, although it has been directed increasingly against North American economic influence in the region. The main problems are those created by industrialization, the rapid increase of population, and the rise of a labour movement within a political system in which the large landowners have long been dominant, and have often ruled through military dictatorships.

The general problems of the underdeveloped countries arise largely from the accelerated pace of industrialization which is sought, and in varying degrees achieved, and which has been provoked to a considerable extent by the example of those countries which are already industrialized; from the rapid growth of population resulting from the improvement of medical care and other welfare services; and from the social and political conditions in which economic development has to take place. The industrialization of the Western countries began, in most cases, in far more favourable conditions of economic organization, political cohesion and stability, and psychological preparation of the population by the decline of traditional institutions, as well as being a more protracted and leisurely process. Quite apart from the economic difficulties which the present underdeveloped countries encounter from the fact that there are already in the world advanced industrial countries, which compete with them in trade and investment, they have also to contend with political instability, with popular demands for high levels of consumption and welfare, and with the powerful opposing forces of traditional ways of life.

In such conditions the importance of elites and leaders who are capable of inspiring effective action, of controlling and directing events, is greatly enhanced. It is further enhanced by the lack of experience in social and political organization of the mass of the population who have in many cases been maintained in subjection and inactivity by autocratic rulers, either indigenous or foreign. Which, then, are the new elites which emerge to initiate or to take over the task of economic development, and how effective is their leadership? Some of the important elite groups have been distinguished in a recent study of industrialization which suggests that "there are five ideal types of elites who customarily and variously take the leadership of the industrialization process ... (1) a dynastic elite; (2) the middle class; (3) the revolutionary intellectuals; (4) the colonial administrators; and (5) the nationalist leaders."[2] Two of these elites have been relatively unimportant in the most recent period and we can deal with their influence very briefly. The colonial administrators created, in many countries of Asia and Africa, some of the prerequisites for industrial development, by establishing an effective administration and judiciary, introducing modern education, and promoting modern banking and commerce, as well as some modern industries.[3] Nevertheless, these achievements could not lead directly to rapid industrialization, for a number of reasons: the economic interests of the colonial power, and the generally inhibiting effects of foreign rule were both serious obstacles, as was the fact that where large-scale commerce and industry did develop it was usually in the hands of the nationals of the colonial power.

In those countries which are still under colonial rule today, it is usually recognized that foreign administrators can do little more than prepare the conditions for economic growth, which can only be prosecuted energetically by new elites after the attainment of independence.

The role of dynastic elites—whether drawn from a landowning or a commercial aristocracy—is also limited. In a few countries of the Middle East and Latin America elites of this kind have made attempts, sometimes under foreign pressure, to bring about social and economic changes from above, but their actions are seriously restricted by the interest which they have as a class in maintaining the existing state of society. In order to carry out successfully their policies of reform they would have to permit, and still more encourage, much greater social mobility, to extend education rapidly, and to make their own elite positions more easily accessible to individuals and groups from the lower strata of society. It is doubtful whether they can do this on the scale and with the speed necessary to meet the urgent demands for economic growth and rising levels of living, or to counter the influence of the new elites which are competing with them for mass support.

The other three elites which I have mentioned play a much more significant role in most of the underdeveloped countries. The middle classes as a whole influence economic development not only by the contribution of their special skills, but by their general commitment to modern ways of living. In the various types of underdeveloped society, different groups within the middle classes may have a more or less predominant influence. In most of the former colonial countries of Asia and Africa the middle classes have been created largely by the educational and administrative systems which the ruling colonial powers introduced, as may be seen particularly clearly in the case of India. An Indian historian, B. B. Misra, in his well-documented account of the growth of the middle classes there, has observed that "the bulk of the Indian middle classes came to consist of the intelligentsia —public servants, other salaried employees, and members of the learned professions."[4] The main reason for this predominance of the intelligentsia in the middle classes was the lack of opportunities for the formation of an indigenous business class, which in turn was due to the low rate of economic growth and to the privileged position of nationals of the colonial power in the small sector of modern industry and commerce. The predominance of the "white collar" middle classes has not been affected significantly by the political independence of these countries, because the planning of economic growth and the concentration of effort upon public rather than private enterprise has offered little scope for the development of a class of businessmen. On the other hand, in the countries of Latin America and the Middle East a business class was created much earlier, and it has formed an important section of the middle classes. For all that, it is not a very effective elite at the present time. The economic situation of most of the Latin-American countries has been deteriorating steadily since 1958, while the population has continued to increase, and this circumstance, together with the association between Latin-American business and the North American firms which have a large share in the raw materials industries, and which have in the past ruthlessly exploited natural resources and exported the profits, has brought discredit upon the business elite. The opposition to the business elite, and to North American business interests, was given a further impetus by the Cuban revolution, and notwithstanding the doubts which the subsequent evolution of Fidel Castro's political doctrines and actions has aroused, it is clear that new elites committed to socialist planning are developing rapidly throughout Latin America.

Within the "white collar" middle class in the majority of underdeveloped countries the most important group is that of the higher government officials, who assume exceptional responsibilities and acquire exceptional power in conditions where economic and social planning is undertaken on such a large scale. In many respects, government officials are to the economic development of the new nations in the twentieth century what the capitalist entrepreneurs were to the economic development of Western societies in the eighteenth and nineteenth centuries. But for all their importance their power is more closely circumscribed. The capitalist entrepreneurs were an independent class whose influence spread through government and administration, while the officials are the subordinates of political leaders; there is no more a managerial or bureaucratic revolution in the underdeveloped countries than there is in the advanced industrial societies.

It is the political elite in the underdeveloped countries which has been pre-eminent in deciding the course of their development. The origins of this elite are to be found, in most cases, in one or other of the two groups mentioned earlier—the nationalist leaders, and the revolutionary intellectuals—which in some cases are associated or merge with one another. In almost all the Asian and African countries intellectuals have taken a prominent part in the struggles against colonial rule. University students were often the shock troops of the independence movements, and those who studied abroad created or helped to create the new nationalist parties. A study of the new Indonesian elites, which deals with the early phases of an independence movement, notes the spread of radical ideas among university students and the strong influence of politically minded intellectuals, and shows that educated Indonesians formed a majority of the active participants in the anti-colonial movements.[5] In Nigeria, a new elite of "Western-educated and frequently self-made men" supplanted the old elite of the traditional ruling families as the independence movement developed (although, as in most cases, there was some overlapping between the old and new elites, since the old elite families were those which had the best opportunities to procure a Western education for their children).[6] T. Hodgkin also points out, in his *African Political Parties*, that nationalistic political elites are recruited very largely from the new "middle classes," and especially from the "educated middle class." In the Ghana House of Assembly, after the 1954 election, 29 per cent of the members were school teachers, 17 per cent clerks, accountants, etc., 17 per cent members of the liberal professions. Among the Legislative Assembly members of the eight territories of the former French West Africa, after the 1957 elections, 22 per cent were teachers, 27 per cent were government officials, and 20 per cent were members of the liberal professions (op. cit., p. 29.)

But nationalist leaders have not always been either intellectuals or revolutionaries. In India, they were neither the one nor the other. True, the National Congress was largely created, and was strongly influenced in its early phases, by intellectuals who had imbibed Western ideas; but they were liberals, not revolutionaries, and their influence was short-lived. It was soon counteracted by the influence of political leaders who came from business communities or the professions, and even more by the moral and social doctrines of Gandhi, which were derived from traditional religious thought.

Where revolutionary intellectuals have attained power it has usually been through the adoption of Marxism as a political creed, and by the formation of Communist parties or similar organizations which brought them into a close association with the industrial workers and especially with the poorer peasants. The appeals of Marxism and Communism in the underdeveloped countries have been well stated by Raymond Aron: ". . . communism may be a progressive force wherever elites are inadequate for their task, either preserving a more or less feudal system of organization, or proceeding too slowly with the capitalist equipment of the country . . . In our day an elite which fails to make use of technical resources to raise the standard of life and increase the wealth of the community is indeed a bankrupt elite. It is natural that a party, representative of the peasants and workers, who are in poverty because the productivity of their labour is low, should come forward to take over from the soldiers, bankers or great landowners who prefer to spend their profits on luxurious American cars rather than on tractors or machine tools."[7]

The appeal of communism is enhanced by the fact that the Communist parties possess, in Marxism, an effective "political formula" (to use Mosca's term[8])—that is, a creed which states clearly the ends to be pursued, and supplies a moral justification of the governing elite and its actions. Marxism appears as a progressive doctrine, a modern view of the world that is irreconcilably opposed to ancient superstitions, an egalitarian creed which has had the power to enthuse men everywhere and most of all in those countries where immense wealth and the most degrading poverty co-exist, and at the same time a theory of rapid industrialization which incites men to activity and labour and which can claim in the economic growth of the USSR a practical confirmation of its truth. Marxism, in this aspect, is the Calvinism of the twentieth-century industrial revolutions. Nevertheless, as we have seen, the intellectuals are not everywhere animated by revolutionary ideas, still less by those of Marxism; and economic development is not in most cases being prosecuted under the leadership of Communist parties. The resistances to Marxism are numerous and they grow both from within Marxist thought itself and from other systems of ideas. As an intellectual scheme, orthodox Marxism today arouses numerous doubts and criticisms, some of which we have considered in an earlier chapter; but more important in the present context is the fact that its perils as a practical creed have been plainly recognized. The experiences of the USSR, which show on one hand the possibilities of rapid economic growth under the leadership of the Communist party, also reveal, as the possible or probable concomitants of this kind of one-party rule, dictatorship and loss of personal liberty, persecution and widespread suffering. It is for these reasons that so many intellectuals in the developing countries have been seeking a new progressive creed, which they have hoped to find, at various times, in African or Asian socialism, or in the doctrines of the Cuban revolutionaries, but which still eludes any precise and compelling formulation.

If we now look at the external influences we can see that in many underdeveloped countries Marxism is opposed both by traditional religious thinkers and by those who have adopted Western liberal ideas. India presents us with an extreme situation in this respect, for although the Communist party there constitutes at present the principal opposition to the ruling Congress Party, the intellectual influence of Marxism, or of any revolutionary ideas, is slight. In India, few of those who can be described as intellectuals in the modern, secular sense are in any consistent, radical or effective way critics of their society, or creators of new social doctrines which can inspire popular action, and for the most part the influence of the intellectuals is assimilated to that of the new middle classes as a whole, whose style of life brings about small and gradual changes in taste and manners. The existence of a hereditary intellectual elite—the Brahmins—from which many of the modern intellectuals come, ensures that they remain attached in manifold ways to the religious and social ideals of the traditional society; and even the recruitment to intellectual occupations from a wider social area, which might tend to diminish this attachment, has so far failed to produce a self-confident, modern intellectual class, which could assume a leading position, because of the divisive forces of caste and regional loyalties. In most of the underdeveloped countries traditional ideas may be less powerful, more compatible with Marxism, than in India; but the influence of revolutionary intellectuals may still be weak, either because there are effective ruling elites which base their policies upon nationalist or liberal doctrines, or because the intellectuals are isolated from the mass of the population by their Western culture. In some situations, intellectuals may not be a politically active group at all, because they are sufficiently few in numbers to be absorbed, in which case they may come to resemble their counterparts in some of the Western societies. But whatever the variations in the situation of the intellectuals—whether they are revolutionary leaders, critics of the elite in power, or men deeply engaged in the specialized activities of education, administration, journalism or the like —they constitute everywhere one of the most important groups in the underdeveloped societies, because these societies live, at the present time, by means of ideas and creeds, which include nationalism, socialism, Marxism, and industrialism; and they can only live and develop in this way now that their traditional institutions have been partially destroyed and cannot be revived.

The leaders of nationalist movements obviously form one of the most important elite groups in the Asian and African countries, where the impetus for economic development came originally from the struggles for political independence. These leaders may be the products of Western universities and radical student movements, of indigenous business and professional communities, or of traditional elite groups, but they resemble each other in the fact that their power derives from leadership of a political party which is based upon, and expresses, nationalist sentiment. The nationalism of the developing countries is a consequence of the struggle for independence from alien rulers, and also of the nature of the problems which confront these countries after independence is gained; especially the need to create or consolidate a nation out of related but still separate tribal or linguistic groups, and the economic need to plan on a national scale the industrial development of the country. It is not surprising to find, then, that in many developing countries a single party which has successfully led the independence movement, establishes itself as the ruling elite and justifies its power both by its past deeds and by its promise to create a modern nation in the future.

This is not to say that nationalism is the only "political formula" which sustains these ruling elites. Other ideas, of democracy, socialism, or welfare, may be incorporated in the ruling doctrine, just as in other cases—in China, for example —nationalist ideas may find their place in a revolutionary ideology. In Africa, nationalism is infused with socialistic doctrines on one hand, and with the ideas of pan-Africanism, taking shape in actual projects of federation, on the other. Similarly, in most of the Asian countries nationalism has a strongly socialistic cast, and in some countries of the Middle East and Latin America the growth of nationalism is associated with socialism by reason of its opposition to foreign business interests. One factor which makes nationalism, by itself, an ambiguous doctrine for the political rulers of the under-developed countries is that it may be backward-looking and seek to revive traditional institutions and traditional elites, especially in those societies which have preserved their own

ancient civilization. In the course of the independence movement there may develop, alongside the political struggle, a
cultural conflict in which the language, values and institutions
of the foreign rulers are rejected while the country's own
ancient glories and accomplishments are lauded and held up
for imitation. A classical instance of this pattern of events
is the revival of Hinduism in India, which was both used and
furthered by Gandhi in creating a mass movement of opposition to British rule; but other instances can be found in
some Arab countries, in Pakistan, and even in some parts of
Africa, where Islam has provided a rallying point for opponents of colonial rule.[9] Where nationalism is associated in
this way with a traditionalist revival of ancient values and
ways of life, it may become an obstacle to economic development, especially by its opposition to a thoroughgoing ration-
alization of social life. Thus, although the nationalist political
leaders have powerful forces on their side—the memories
and rituals of the struggle for independence, the desire to
create a viable nation and the compelling need for national
planning of economic life—they also confront serious
difficulties, which arise from the conflict between traditional-
ists and modernists within their own ranks and in the society
at large, from the lack of precision and coherence in the
doctrines upon which they base, in part, their authority,
and from the moral deterioration which is likely to occur
among the leading cadres and officials of the ruling party in
a one-party system of government, in so far as the actions
of individuals are not strictly controlled either by a traditional
code of behaviour or by a clear and vigorous social doctrine.

There is another social group which we have not so far
mentioned, but which has been, in some developing societies,
more influential than either the intellectuals or the political
leaders—the military officers. It is evident that in newly

independent countries, where political institutions are still in the making and political authority is still, in varying degrees, unsettled and insecure, those who control the ultimate power of direct physical coercion have the opportunity to play an important part in deciding the future of the nation. Whether they will in fact intervene in political affairs depends upon many factors: the traditions in which the military officers have been educated, their social origins, the extent of their influence over the troops they command, and on the other side, the strength of the political leaders and the character of their relations with the military chiefs.[10] In the past, some of the principal examples of military intervention in politics have occurred in the Latin American countries, but these are not altogether relevant in considering the present situation. They occurred mainly in the period before rapid economic growth began, and the *caudillos* with their armed bands resembled feudal barons, reacting to the breakdown of a settled political authority, rather than the kind of elite bent upon industrialization and economic growth with which we are here concerned.[11] This is, of course, one of the ways in which military chiefs may still come to power, but at the present time there are also other factors which may enhance their importance. A recent writer observes that the military have become the dominant group in at least eight of the African and Asian countries, and suggests that the political role of the army in the developing countries should be considered ". . . first, with respect to the political implications of the army as a modern institution that has been somewhat artificially introduced into disorganized transitional societies: and second, with respect to the role that such an army can play in shaping attitudes toward modernity in other spheres of society."[12] Armies, as he points out, are among the most modern elements in the underdeveloped countries, and are imbued with "the spirit of rapid technological change." At the same time, they are an important modernizing influence upon the society at large, for they train their members in modern techniques and inculcate new attitudes to work.

There is another characteristic of these new armies to which a number of writers have drawn attention; namely that they constitute or have constituted until recently, one of the most effective channels of upward social mobility. In those societies in which higher education has been accessible only to the upper class, and in which the political leaders have also been drawn largely from this class—as is the case in many of the Middle Eastern states—the army has provided an opportunity for a new elite to form, recruited from the middle strata of society, and often allying itself with the peasantry and working class, and to engage in a struggle for political ascendancy. In Egypt, Syria, and Iraq, revolutions have been led by young army officers who belonged in the main to the middle class and lower middle class. And in Latin America, too, military intervention in politics has taken on a new form during the present century: the pattern is no longer simply that of the *caudillo* who belongs to or aspires to the landowning upper class and seizes power in a factional struggle; there have also been popular revolutions led by the young officers. As Lieuwen says: "In a number of Latin-American countries . . . the pattern of revolution underwent radical change in the second quarter of the twentieth century. . . . The general picture was one in which the young officers, also frustrated in their ambitions, made common cause with the rising popular groups. Together they collaborated in bringing down, by force, the *ancien régime*."[13]

We see from this short review of the situation in the underdeveloped countries that there are several elite groups which may engage in the struggle for leadership: the revolutionary intellectuals, the nationalist political leaders, and the military officers. Other groups, such as the government officials and the businessmen, may also acquire a considerable influence in directing the course of economic growth. What factors determine which of these groups shall take the leading role? In some cases, in Latin America and the Middle East, dynastic elites of landowners or businessmen have established themselves in an earlier period and are difficult to dislodge, even though their rule is ineffective and obstructs economic growth. Military intervention may be favoured in some countries by a tradition of military rule, as in Latin America, or by a cultural tradition which does not emphasize the separation of military and political functions, as may be the case in Islamic countries; or it may be discouraged by a strongly established doctrine of military neutrality, as is possible in those countries which were formerly under British rule.

The creation of a close bond between the elite and the rest of the population, through such intermediaries as trade unions, peasant organizations and mass political parties, in order that the elite can be seen to express the aspirations of the people and to promote their interests, appears to be a crucial factor in the successful development of these countries. This condition marks a difference between the process of economic and social development at the present time and that which took place earlier in the Western world. In most of the Western countries, at least up to the middle of the nineteenth century, new elites could form themselves and contend for power without relying upon widespread popular support, or could acquire such support as they needed without being accountable to the mass of the people for their aims and accomplishments. In the present underdeveloped countries the need for popular support arises in great measure from the example of those countries which are already industrialized, and which have high living standards and elaborate provision of social welfare.

The whole process of economic development has become more deliberate and self-conscious than it was in the first industrial revolution. We can point to the contrast in one way by saying that Marxism is *not* the Calvinism of the twentieth-century industrial revolutions. Calvinism was a theological creed which, if we are to follow Max Weber's account, produced unintended consequences in economic and social life by inculcating the values of regular, sustained work and of thrift and abstinence. Marxism is a social science, and at the same time a social and political creed, which sets out directly a vision of a future condition of human society and a programme of action to realize it. But Marxism only displays these features in an especially striking form; in great measure, all the doctrines which shape the plans and policies of the underdeveloped countries invoke an ideal conception of society—a classless society, a welfare state, a co-operative commonwealth—which includes much more than an industrial economy, although the development of industry is presented as the chief and essential condition for achieving it. The success of the various elites in bringing about rapid economic growth depends, therefore, to a very large extent upon their success in arousing popular enthusiasm, and upon the extent of the support which they can get from major social classes such as the poorer peasants and the industrial workers.

The attempts to win such support, and to draw large numbers of people into the political and social activities of development, can be observed in a great variety of forms, from the creation of mass parties to the organization of agricultural co-operatives and the establishment of community development schemes. There remains the difficulty that in many of the underdeveloped countries the elites are very widely separated from the rest of the people, by their Western education, by their origins in higher castes, in landowning or business families, or in the families of tribal chiefs, and by their whole style of life. This situation presents the danger that some kind of authoritarian elite rule will grow up, especially when we consider the long habituation of the people in these countries to such forms of rule. At the same time, the prominence attributed to, or acquired by, small elite groups partly defeats the purposes of planned economic growth, by excluding or discouraging enterprising individuals in the lower, and traditionally submissive, strata of society. An example is to be found in the community development programmes in several countries, and notably in India, which have been only moderately successful in eliciting popular participation in development activities,[14] and have come under the predominant influence of higher castes or wealthy landowners. Nevertheless, community development does provide some opportunities for groups at the bottom of the social hierarchy to assert their own interests, and it also provides administrative posts at the lower levels to which individuals from these groups can aspire, and in which they can gain experience in the business of government. Similar opportunities, on a wider scale, are created by the expansion of education, and it is probably this last development, together with the example conveyed by the advanced industrial countries, which has done most to stimulate and form the aspirations of the mass of the people.

In spite of the great prominence which elites, and even individual leaders, attain in the underdeveloped countries—partly by the contrast which they present with the backwardness of the general population—it is not, in the last resort, the activities of these elites and leaders alone which can decide the success, or determine the form, of the course of development upon which they have entered. Of course, the elites and leaders must be capable and efficient; but that is not enough. They must also express adequately, and pursue steadfastly, the ideals of those social classes which constitute the great majority of the population and which are struggling at the present time to escape from their age-old confinement to a life of poverty and subservience.

## NOTES

1 The proportion of the population in urban areas ranges between 60–65 per cent in Argentina and Chile, and 36 per cent in Brazil.

2 Clark Kerr, John T. Dunlop, Frederick H. Harbison and Charles A. Myers, *Industrialism and Industrial Man*, Chap. 3. "The Industrializing Elites and their Strategies", p. 50.

3 I mention here the actual achievements of colonial administrators. I do not mean to assert that similar developments could not have taken place indigenously if there had not been colonial conquests, although in many cases this seems to me doubtful.

4 B. B. Misra, *The Indian Middle Classes*, p. 343.

5 W. Van Niel, *The Modern Indonesian Elite*.

6 H. H. Smythe and M. M. Smythe, *The New Nigerian Elite*.

7 Raymond Aron, "Social Structure and the Ruling Class", *British Journal of Sociology*, I (2), 1950, p. 135.

8 Mosca, op. cit., p. 70. ". . . ruling classes do not justify their power exclusively by de facto possession of it, but try to find a moral and legal basis for it, representing it as the logical and necessary consequence of doctrines and beliefs that are generally recognized and accepted . . . This legal and moral basis, or principle, on which the power of the political class rests, is what we have elsewhere called . . . the 'political formula.' "

9 For example, a study of Senegal before independence observes that ". . . the power and influence of the traditional political chiefs has to a large extent been transferred to the Khalifas of the great Islamic sects; the latter represent today the principal force capable of resisting the modernist elite, and one with which the latter and the political movements identified with it must to some extent come to terms". P. Mercier, "Evolution of Senegalese Elites", *International Social Science Bulletin*, VIII (3), 1956.

10 For a general discussion of the factors involved see S. E. Finer, *The Man on Horseback*; and especially Chaps. 8 and 9 on the underdeveloped countries.

11 Edwin Lieuwen, *Arms and Politics in Latin America*, Part I.

12 Lucian W. Pye, "Armies in the Process of Political Modernization", *European Journal of Sociology*, II (1), 1961, p. 83.

13 Edwin Lieuwen, op. cit., p. 132. The examples given are Bolivia in 1936, Guatemala in 1944, Argentina in 1943 and Colombia in 1953.

14 See, for example, the United Nations study, *Community Development and Economic Development* (Bangkok, 1960).

# VI

## DEMOCRACY AND THE PLURALITY OF ELITES

THE criticism of democratic theories of politics which Mosca and Pareto formulated in the theory of elites began with the observation that in every society there is a minority which effectively rules. This criticism could be met—as Mosca himself saw—while acknowledging the fact that a governing elite is necessary in every society, by arguing that the distinctive feature of democracy, as a form of government, is that it permits elites to form freely, and establishes a regulated competition between elites for the positions of power. This conception of democracy as a political system in which political parties compete for the votes of a mass electorate, implies further that the elites are relatively "open" and are recruited on the basis of merit (i.e. there is presumed to be a continuous and extensive circulation of elites), and that the mass of the population is able to participate in ruling society at least in the sense that it can exercise a choice between the rival elites. Karl Mannheim, as we saw earlier, had originally connected elite theories with Fascism and with anti-intellectualist doctrines of "direct action," but came later to hold a view of this kind: ". . . the actual shaping of policy is in the hands of elites; but this does not mean that the society is not democratic. For it is sufficient for democracy that the individual citizens, though prevented from taking a direct part in government all the time, have at least the *possibility* of making their aspirations felt at certain intervals . . . Pareto is right in

stressing that political power is always exercised by minorities (elites), and we may also accept Robert Michels' law of
the trend towards oligarchic rule in party organizations.
Nevertheless, it would be wrong to over-estimate the
stability of such elites in democratic societies, or their ability
to wield power in arbitrary ways. In a democracy, the
governed can always act to remove their leaders or to force
them to take decisions in the interests of the many."[1] Mannheim also emphasized the importance of selection by merit,
and of the reduced distance between elites and masses in
creating a compatibility between elite rule and democratic
government: "We assume that democracy is characterized,
not by the absence of all elite strata, but rather by a new mode
of elite selection and a new self-interpretation of the elite ...
What changes most of all in the course of democratization
is the distance between the elite and the rank-and-file. The
democratic elite has a mass background; this is why it can
mean something for the mass."[2]

The reconciliation between the idea of elites and the idea
of democratic government has proceeded apace during the
twentieth century, as Mannheim's own work bears witness,
and it has been assisted by a number of favourable circumstances. One of these is the general enhancement of the
importance of leadership which has resulted from large-scale
warfare, from international rivalry in economic growth and
from the rise and development of new nations; all of which
has turned men's thoughts away from the dangers of elite
rule towards the need for efficient and enterprising elites.
Another circumstance which has lent support to the competition model of democracy is the contrast between the
consequences of elite rule in one-party states, and the experiences of those democratic societies in which there is competition for power among several political parties, none of
which aims to bring about a radical change in the social

structure. Furthermore, this model has also a scientific appeal, by reason of the analogy which it presents to the model of economic behaviour in a free enterprise system, and of the promise which it thus holds out of an analysis of political behaviour as exact and rigorous, if also as limited, as economic analysis. The analogy was stated plainly by Schumpeter,[3] who also went on to argue, more generally, that modern democracy arose with the capitalist economic system and is causally connected with it.[4] The view is conveyed succinctly in the remark made by a successful politician, which Schumpeter quotes: "What businessmen do not understand is that exactly as they are dealing in oil so I am dealing in votes."[5] More recently, this conception of democracy as a competition for votes between political parties has been presented in more elaborate forms, as for example in the "economic theory of democracy" of A. Downs, who summarizes his theory in the following terms: "Our main thesis is that parties in democratic politics are analogous to entrepreneurs in a profit-seeking economy. So as to attain their private ends, they formulate whatever policies they believe will gain the most votes, just as entrepreneurs produce whatever products they believe will gain the most profits for the same reasons."[6] Another example of the use of this model is to be found in the tentative efforts to apply the theory of games to political behaviour, i.e. to apply to the activities of political parties a mathematical scheme which is extensively used in analysing the behaviour of business enterprises.[7]

But it is not only the competition between political parties which serves to reconcile the existence of elites with democracy. The advocates of this view discover a more general system of checks and balances in the plurality of elites which characterizes democratic societies. Raymond Aron has presented the case in a cogent and revealing manner: ". . . although there are everywhere business managers, government officials, trade union secretaries and ministers, they are not everywhere recruited in the same way and they may either form one coherent whole or remain comparatively distinct from one another. The fundamental difference between a society of the Soviet type and one of the Western type is that the former has a unified elite and the latter a divided elite. In the USSR the trade union secretaries, the business managers and the higher officials generally belong to the Communist party . . . On the other hand, democratic societies, which I would rather call pluralistic societies, are full of the noise of public strife between the owners of the means of production, trade union leaders and politicians. As all are entitled to form associations, professional and political organizations abound, each one defending its members' interests with passionate ardour. Government becomes a business of compromises. Those in power are well aware of their precarious position. They are considerate of the opposition because they themselves have been, and will one day again be, in opposition."[8]

The definition of democracy as competition between elites may be criticized on various grounds—that it is excessively arbitrary and leaves out of account generally recognized characteristics of the phenomenon which it defines, or that the theory in which it is used is inadequate or untrue, or that it proceeds from a set of value judgments to which other value judgments can be opposed. Modern democracy has most often, and by most political thinkers, been defined as the participation of the mass of the people in government, and one of its classical formulations is that of Lincoln's Gettysburg Address: "government of the people, by the people, for the people." All elite theories deny that there can be, in any real sense, government *by* the people.[9] The denial may be founded, as in the case of Pareto and Mosca, upon the somewhat trivial observation that in most known societies of the past there has been a clear distinction between the rulers and the ruled, or it may rest upon a more theoretical analysis, as in the writings of Michels, Mannheim, and Aron, which seeks to show that in any large and complex society (and in large and complex organizations within society) democracy can only be *representative*, not direct, and that the representatives are a minority who clearly possess greater political power than those whom they represent, since the influence of the latter is confined to passing judgment, at fairly long intervals, upon the activities of the minority. But several objections can be brought against this analysis. In the first place, according to the view of democracy which we are now considering, the system of government by represent-ation is quite clearly regarded as an imperfect realization of democracy, in so far as it does permanently exclude the many from any experience of government. The undemocratic character of representative government becomes most apparent when the representative principle is applied in a system of indirect election, whereby an elected elite itself elects a second elite which is endowed with equal or superior political power. This device has often been resorted to by the opponents of popular rule—a recent example is to be found in the constitution of the Fifth Republic in France under the leadership of de Gaulle—and de Tocqueville, among others, saw in it an effective means of restricting democracy. Even when the defenders of the idea of democracy as com-petition between elites do not propound it deliberately as a defence against democracy in its other sense—against that incursion of the masses into politics which de Tocqueville, Pareto, Mosca and Ortega y Gasset unite in deploring—they are still inclined to take representative government as the ideal, instead of measuring it against the ideal of direct participation by the people in legislation and administration and looking about for means by which this end might be more closely approached.

This argument suggests a second objection to the analysis of democracy which Schumpeter, Aron and others provide. According to their accounts democracy is to be conceived as something accomplished and complete, which can be contrasted straightforwardly with other types of political system. On the other hand, in the conception of democracy as government *by* the people which prevailed during most of the nineteenth century, democracy was conceived as a continuing process in which political rights, the power to influence decisions on social policy, were progressively extended to groups in the population which had formerly been deprived of them. This implies two things: first, that democracy appeared primarily as a doctrine and political movement of the lower classes of society against the dominance of the aristocratic and wealthy classes (and this is, of course, one of the main causes which provoked the response of the elite theories); and second, that it was regarded as a movement towards an ideal condition of society in which men would be fully self-governing, which might never be completely achieved, but which democrats ought to strive for. It would not have occurred to most of the democratic political thinkers of the nineteenth century to regard universal suffrage, competition between several political parties and representative government, however valuable by contrast with the institutions of other political regimes, as the ultimate point of democratic progress, beyond which it was impossible to venture.

The reasons for the emergence, in the twentieth century, of a static conception of democracy in which elite rule is sanctioned by periodic elections, have to be sought in the political circumstances of this century. It was the establishment of one-party states, in a Fascist form in Germany and Italy, and in a Communist form in the USSR, which gave point and credibility to the identification of democracy with a multi-party, representative system. The passage which I quoted earlier from Raymond Aron, in which the unified elite in Soviet-type societies is contrasted with the plurality of elites in Western-type societies, makes this perfectly clear. We may, however, question whether organized political parties—and more broadly, organized elite groups—are necessary or sufficient for the existence of a democratic system of government. It has often been held that they are not necessary, and that, for example, in a more decentralized type of political system than those which now exist in most nations, the selection of the political leaders for the time being might be accomplished through the activities of associations which would be less highly organized, less bureaucratic and less permanent than the present-day political parties. To this should be added that in a society from which social classes had been eliminated (which many thinkers have envisaged as a consequence of the growth of democracy) the most important single basis for the formation of parties would likewise have disappeared; and although it is not impossible to think of other social distinctions which might engender political parties, it is difficult to conceive that such parties would have the same scope and influence in political life as those with which we are familiar now. This argument refers, it will be noted, to a political system without any political parties, and not to a one-party regime. The latter is not democratic at all, for it deprives the individual, confronted by the ruling party, of any real possibility of expressing or giving effect to his disagreement with important social decisions, since he lacks any forum in which to expound his own opinions or to discover the opinions of his fellows, in the shape of an autonomous and powerful association. It may well be that in periods of popular enthusiasm a single party does express the purpose of the great majority of a nation, and succeeds in drawing large numbers of people, without compulsion, into the activities of legislation and administration; but in that case there can be no need for it to suppress such other political parties as still survive. It may also be that the rule of a single party can be justified by the necessities of war, of rapid industrialization, or of the creation of a new nation out of a former colonial territory, but that does not make the political regime in which it functions a democratic one. If the necessity can be demonstrated, the ruling party may be regarded as governing *for* the people, but it is not the case that the people govern themselves.

A discussion of whether political parties are *necessary* to a democratic system of government must remain unavoidably speculative, and it is both easier and more practical to consider whether the competition between parties and elites is *sufficient* to ensure democracy. There are many liberal thinkers today who would assert that it is sufficient, or who would at least regard the competition between elites as being so important as to absolve them from further inquiry into the conditions of democracy. They would have the support of Karl Mannheim who, as we have seen, claimed that what made a society democratic was simply that individual citizens should have "at least the *possibility* of making their aspirations felt at certain intervals."[10] On the other hand, Schumpeter and Aron both pay much attention to other influences upon the political system. Schumpeter sets out explicitly what he terms "conditions for the success of the democratic method," which he classifies under four headings: (i) that the human material of politics (i.e. the elites) should be of sufficiently high quality; (ii) that the effective range of political decision should not be extended too far; (iii) that the government should be able to command the services of a well-trained bureaucracy of good standing and tradition; and (iv) that there should be democratic self-control, i.e. that the competing elites should tolerate each other's rule and should resist the offerings of crooks and cranks, while the electorate, having made its choice, should refrain from interfering incessantly in the political actions of its representatives. Similarly, Aron, in the article cited earlier, states three conditions for the success of the contemporary pluralistic democracies: (i) the restoration of government authority capable of settling the disputes between groups and enforcing the decisions necessary in the community's joint interest; (ii) an efficient economic administration which will preserve mobility and revive incentives; and (iii) a limitation of the influence of those individuals and groups which want to change the whole framework of society. It is obvious, however, that these accounts remain within the scheme of ideas which sees democracy as competition between elites, and explore its further implications, while they neglect many other factors which influence the success or failure, and the extent, of democracy in a larger sense. I shall examine first some of the other political influences. It has been very generally assumed—it is assumed, for example, by Mannheim, although this does not accord well with his other pronouncements on the conditions for democracy—that the development of a democratic polity requires, in addition to the competition between elites, changes in the structure and composition of elites, in their self-conceptions, and in their relations with the rest of the population. Briefly, it seems to be assumed that in a democracy there will be a more rapid and extensive movement of individuals into and out of the elites, that there will be an increasing number of elite positions in relation to the population as a whole, that the elites will develop a less "aristocratic" outlook and will regard themselves as being closely linked with the masses, and that, in consequence of various levelling influences they will actually be closer to the masses in their style of life. The first two of these conditions would bring about a situation in which a far greater number of individuals had the experience of ruling as well as of being ruled, while the other conditions would change the character of political rule in some measure, making it less remote, authoritarian, majestic and irresistible. If we now look at the Western democracies of the present day we shall see that, while they conform well with the competition model of democracy, they are deficient in respect of these other conditions: there is not a rapid circulation of the personnel of the elites, which are still recruited predominantly from the upper class in society;[11] the outlook of the elites has changed only slowly and the old aristocratic view of their functions is kept alive by their recruitment from the upper class, by the elite theories themselves, and by the prevailing social doctrines of "getting on" and reaching "the top"; and lastly, the "levelling" of conditions in Western societies has gone on so slowly that the rulers are still very sharply distinguished, economically and socially, from the ruled. It should be noted, too, that the political parties which stand at the centre of the competition between elites have themselves lost something of their democratic character with their transformation into mass parties. They may not have become, in most cases, quite the oligarchic organizations which Michels foresaw,[12] but they are more easily dominated by their officials, and it is correspondingly more difficult for the rank and file members to have an effective influence in the shaping of policy.

Besides these political factors, we should also consider whether there are not more general social conditions which are essential to the life and growth of a democratic system of government. It is a notable feature of the recent elite theories that, having defined democracy as simply a *form of government of a whole society*, and thus excluded from the definition any non-political factors such as appear, for example, in the notions of "social democracy," or "industrial democracy," they go on to eliminate so far as possible even a consideration of the influence which factors of this kind may have upon the form of government itself. But this is to overlook or reject a fundamental idea of sociology—namely, that the institutions which exist in the different spheres of society are not merely co-existent but are connected with each other by relations of concordance or contradiction and mutually affect each other—which was admirably formulated by Marx, in his criticism of the political philosophers of his day, when he argued that it was a profound error to separate man as a citizen (i.e. as an individual with political rights) completely from man as a member of civil society (i.e. as an individual engaged in family life and in economic production).[13] Are we to suppose, for instance, that the modern democratic family in Western societies, which has been exhaustively described by many sociologists, and in which the relations between the members are, generally speaking, more co-operative and less authoritarian than was the case in the nineteenth century, has come into being unaffected by democratic ideas of government; or that once it exists it has no significance for the maintenance and extension of democratic attitudes and practices in the sphere of government? Can we accept that democratic government, which requires of the individual independent judgment and active participation in deciding important social issues, will flourish when in one of the most important spheres of life—that of work and economic production—the great majority of individuals are denied the opportunity to take an effective part in reaching the decisions which vitally affect their lives? It does not seem to me that a man can live in a condition of complete and unalterable subordination during much of his life, and yet acquire the habits of responsible choice and self-government which political democracy calls for. It is true that in the

Western societies the subordination of the individual at work is less onerous than it used to be in some respects; the individual worker has some influence upon his working conditions through his trade union and through institutions of joint consultation which have developed in a rudimentary fashion, while the substantial increase in leisure time has enlarged the sphere in which he is able to decide things for himself. On the other hand, much industrial work has become more subdivided and repetitive in modern times, with the result that the worker, even if he is not subjected to the old type of authoritarian control by his employer, still finds less and less opportunity to exercise judgment, imagination, or skill in the performance of his task.[14]

There are other circumstances, more frequently discussed, which affect the practice of democratic government. Great inequalities of wealth and income plainly influence the extent to which individuals can participate in the activities of ruling the community. A rich man may have difficulty in entering the kingdom of heaven, but he will find it relatively easy to get into the higher councils of a political party, or into some branch of government. He can also exert an influence on political life in other ways: by controlling media of communication, by making acquaintances in the higher circles of politics, by taking a prominent part in the activities of pressure groups and advisory bodies of one kind or another. A poor man has none of these advantages: he has no relationships with influential people, he has little time or energy to devote to political activity, and little opportunity to acquire a thorough knowledge of political ideas or facts. The differences which originate in economic inequalities are enhanced by educational differences. In most of the Western democracies the kind of education provided for those classes which mainly provide the rulers of the community is sharply differentiated from that which is provided for the more numerous class of those who are ruled.[15] The educational system in most Western societies does not only consolidate the distinction between rulers and ruled; it keeps alive and flourishing the whole ideology of elite rule in so far as it emphasizes the selection of exceptional individuals for elite positions, and the rewards in income or status of scholastic achievement, rather than the raising of the general level of education throughout the community and the contribution which this might make to increasing the participation of the mass of citizens in government. The differences of wealth and education which I have mentioned are aspects of the division of society into classes; and it is this fundamental division which has often been regarded, in the theories of "social democracy" for example, as incompatible with democratic government. I shall discuss it further in the following chapter.

The objections which I have so far presented to the elite theories of democracy are based upon an alternative conception of democracy as "government by the people"; but there are other objections which arise from inconsistencies within the elite theories themselves. First, there is the question as to whether any form of government could survive for long if there were permanent opposition and conflict between elites, and an incessant circulation of their personnel. Mannheim, writing on the problems of political democracy in terms of the German situation of the early 1930s, observed that the growth of democracy means a loss of homogeneity in the governing elite and went on to say: "Modern democracy often breaks down because it is burdened with far more complex decision problems than those facing early democratic (or pre-democratic) societies with their more homogeneous ruling groups."[16] T. S. Eliot, in *Notes Towards the Definition of Culture* has argued in a similar fashion that elites, which require a regular circulation of their personnel, are unable to ensure social continuity in the way that the ruling classes of earlier times could do.[17] However, both writers exaggerate the dangers arising from these sources, for there is not at the present time any substantial circulation of individuals between the elites and the rest of the population, and the elites are not as a rule engaged in serious conflict with each other. As Aron says, in discussing the present situation of the Western societies: "The composition of the governing elite may be progressively altered, the relative importance of the various groups in the elite may be changed, but a society can only survive and prosper if there is true collaboration between those groups. In one way or another there must be unity of opinion and action on essential points in the elite."[18] In fact, this unity of opinion and action—and the social continuity which Eliot desires—is largely assured in the Western societies by the recruitment of elites from the upper class of society, and by the ideological support of the theory of elites itself. It is still true that "From the hour of their birth some are marked out for subjection and some for command".[19] In the Western societies the elites stand, for the most part, on one side of the great barrier constituted by class divisions; and so an entirely misleading view of political life is created if we concentrate our attention upon the competition between elites, and fail to examine the conflicts between classes and the ways in which elites are connected with the various social classes.

It is one of the political myths of our age that democracy is protected and sustained principally or solely by the competition between elites, which balance and limit each other's power. When we look at the arguments of the elite theorists in favour of this thesis we find a second inconsistency, which consists in moving, at different stages of the argument, from the concept of a plurality of elites to the quite different concept of a multiplicity of voluntary associations. Mosca, for example, referred to the possibility, in a democratic system, for many different "social forces" (not elites) to take part in political life and to limit the power of other social forces, and especially bureaucracy. Similarly, Aron, when he urges the importance of the diffusion of power in the pluralistic democracies does not invoke only the principal elites which he has distinguished, but speaks of the great variety of professional and political organizations which are to be found in such societies, and which set bounds to the power of the rulers. But this advocacy of flourishing voluntary associations as a vital condition for effective democracy does not lend support to the elite theories. For what is being asserted, when the importance of vigorous local government, professional associations and other voluntary and autonomous bodies is given such prominence, is not that those organizations are elites which are engaged in major struggles for political power, but that they provide so many occasions and opportunities for ordinary men and women to learn and practise the business of self-government. They are means through which government *by* the people is made more real and practical in a large, complex society.

Thus we are led by this path also to the view expressed earlier, that the preservation, and especially the development and improvement, of a democratic system of government does not depend primarily upon fostering the competition between small elite groups whose activities are carried on in realms far removed from the observation or control of ordinary citizens, but upon creating and establishing the conditions in which a large majority of citizens, if not all citizens, can take part in deciding those social issues which vitally affect their individual lives—at work, in the local community, and in the nation—and in which the distinction between elites and masses is reduced to the smallest possible degree. Such a view implies, first, that opportunities to extend the scope of self-government should be assiduously sought, especially in the sphere of economic production, where some modern experiments such as the workers' councils in Yugoslavia, and the community development projects in India, for all the difficulties that they encounter, deserve serious attention; and second, that the present hindrances to full participation in the government of voluntary associations, which arise in the main from differences of social class, and are apparent in the predominance of upper class and middle class individuals as officials of such organizations, should in some way be overcome.

## NOTES

[1] Karl Mannheim, *Essays on the Sociology of Culture*, p. 179.

[2] Ibid., p. 200.

[3] In *Capitalism, Socialism and Democracy*, Chap. XXII, "Another Theory of Democracy". See also above, p. 10.

[4] Ibid., pp. 296–7.

[5] Ibid., p. 285.

[6] A. Downs, *An Economic Theory of Democracy*, pp. 295–6.

[7] Up to the present, however, the theory of games has been used most extensively in the study of international conflicts, notably in the currently fashionable "war-games." Its uses in this field are critically examined in Raymond Aron, *Paix et Guerre entre les nations*, Note finale, "Stratégie rationnelle et politique raisonnable", pp. 751–70.

[8] Raymond Aron, "Social Structure and the Ruling Class", *British Journal of Sociology*, I (1), p. 10.

[9] Raymond Aron, in the article quote above, says that "it is quite impossible for the government of a society to be in the hands of any but a few . . . there is government *for* the people; there is no government *by* the people."

[10] Although he went on, somewhat inconsistently, to discuss the growth of equality and the reduction in the distance between elites and masses as factors in the development of modern democracy.

[11] See above, Chap. III. See also W. L. Guttsman, *The British Political Elite*, Chap. XI, where it is shown how few individuals are enabled to take part in the formulation of national policies. In Britain there is a small group of "the good and the great"—at most a few thousand people, drawn predominantly from the upper class in society—who participate in the work of advisory committees, Royal Commissions, and similar public bodies.

12 Robert Michels, *Political Parties.*

13 Karl Marx, *On the Jewish Question.*

14 See, on these questions, Georges Friedmann, *The Anatomy of Work.*

15 In Britain, the typical careers of upper-class and working-class children may be described as follows: children of the upper class are educated in the major public schools and at the universities of Oxford and Cambridge, whence they proceed into business, politics, the administrative class of the civil service, or the older professions; working-class children are educated in state schools, for the most part secondary modern schools, from which they go at the age of fifteen, into manual jobs in industry or into minor clerical jobs, though some (a higher proportion today than twenty-five years ago) attend grammar schools and may go on to higher education in a provincial university or college of technology. Some children in each class may escape their fate, but the proportion who do so is too small to affect the general picture. The educational situation in the USA differs radically from that in Britain and other European countries, although the change is comparatively recent; there, a very high proportion (some 90 per cent) of the relevant age group in all classes receives secondary education up to the age of seventeen and a still considerable proportion (about 35 per cent) goes on to take a university course.

16 Karl Mannheim, *Essays on the Sociology of Culture.*

17 T. S. Eliot, *Notes Towards the Definition of Culture.* Eliot criticizes Mannheim's view that elites in modern societies can perform adequately the functions of earlier ruling classes without noticing that Mannheim himself had already formulated the criticism. In fact, Mannheim seems never to have reached a settled view of the place of elites in modern society. Sometimes he argues in favour of the competition between elites as a safeguard of democracy; at other times, he advocates rule by a single elite composed of the intellectuals; and finally he suggests that no elite, or group of elites, can ensure political stability unless it takes on the characteristics of a ruling class, possibly by association with an existing upper class, and becomes a hereditary and property-owning group. The only conception which Mannheim consistently excludes is that of a classless, egalitarian society.

18 Raymond Aron, "Social Structure and the Ruling Class", *British Journal of Sociology,* I (2), p. 129.

19 Aristotle, *Politics.*

# VII

## EQUALITY OR ELITES?

DEMOCRACY, in one of its established meanings, implies that
there should be a substantial degree of equality among men,
both in the sense that all the adult members of a society
ought to have, so far as is possible, an equal influence upon
those decisions which affect important aspects of the life of
the society, and in the sense that inequalities of wealth, of
social rank, or of education and access to knowledge, should
not be so considerable as to result in the permanent subordination of some groups of men to others in any of the
various spheres of social life, or to create great inequalities
in the actual exercise of political rights. The advocates of
equality have never been concerned to claim anything so
foolish as that individuals are exactly alike or equal in phy-
sique, intelligence, or character. They have based their case
upon a variety of other considerations, among which there
are three which have a particular importance. The first is that
for all their individual idiosyncrasies, human beings are
remarkably alike in some fundamental respects: they have
similar physical, emotional and intellectual needs. That is
why there can be a science of nutrition, and in a less exact
way, sciences of mental health and healing, and of the education of children. Furthermore, the range of variation in the
qualities of individuals is relatively narrow, and there is a
clustering about the middle of the range. If this were not so
—if there were truly differences of kind, rather than of

degree, among men; if there were brute beasts at one extreme and angels or god-like beings at the other—then one of the factual supports of the egalitarian case would be removed.

The second point is that the individual differences among men and the social distinctions between them are two separate things. Long ago, Rousseau made this important distinction: "I conceive that there are two kinds of inequality among the human species; one, which I call natural or physical, because it is established by nature, and consists in a difference of age, health, bodily strength, and the qualities of the mind or of the soul: and another, which may be called moral or political inequality, because it depends upon a kind of convention, and is established, or at least authorized, by the consent of men. This latter consists of the different privileges, which some men enjoy to the prejudice of others; such as that of being more rich, more honoured, more powerful or even in a position to exact obedience."[1] We cannot tell with any certainty how far these two kinds of inequality have been in correspondence in most of the societies which have existed up to modern times. The theory of the circulation of elites was intended in part to suggest that they were; that the most able individuals in every society succeeded in entering the elite, or in forming a new elite which in due course became pre-eminent. But we have seen earlier that the historical evidence produced in support of this thesis is quite inconclusive, and that the more abundant evidence available in the case of modern societies (which are generally regarded as displaying an exceptional degree of social mobility) does not confirm it. The major inequalities in society are in the main social products, created and maintained by the institutions of property and inheritance, of political and military power, and supported by particular beliefs and doctrines, even though they are never entirely resistant to the ambitions of outstanding individuals.

These considerations lead on to the third point which I have to make about the character of the egalitarian arguments. If neither inequality nor equality is a natural phenomenon, which men have simply to accept, the advocacy of one or the other does not consist in the presentation of a scientific argument based wholly upon matters of fact, but in the formulation of a moral and social ideal. We can *opt* for equality, and although in so doing we have to pay attention to matters of fact which bear upon the practicability of the ideal and upon the means appropriate for attaining it, the ultimate justification for our option is not itself any matter of fact but a reasoned claim that the pursuit of equality is likely to create a more admirable society. In using the term "we" I mean to refer specifically to men living in the societies of the twentieth century; for it was difficult in any earlier age to form a practical conception of a stable and durable egalitarian form of society, given the insecurity of economic life, the absence of effective means of communication, the inadequacy of education, and the lack of knowledge about social structure and individual character. The twentieth century is unique in offering to men for the first time the opportunity and the means to fashion social life according to their desires; and it is both hopeful and terrible for that reason.

It is not my purpose here to set out the moral case for equality,[2] but rather to consider the social and political problems which beset the pursuit of equality, and the criticisms, other than moral objections, which the elite theories bring against it. It will be convenient to begin by examining Marx's conception of a "classless society," both because it presents the ideal of equality in a form which is more widely accepted than any other in the modern world, and because it was the principal source from which, by opposition, the elite theories themselves arose. Everyone knows that Marx did not write a blue print for the socialist society which he envisaged and desired[3]; nevertheless, it is unmistakably clear from those of his writings which refer to the future socialist society, what he regarded, in broad outline, as its distinctive features. Marx's sketch of the classless society incorporates moral, sociological and historical elements. The moral aspect is treated most fully in some of his early manuscripts, and particularly in the *Economic and Philosophical Manuscripts* of 1844,[4] but it is by no means neglected in his later writings.[5] From this aspect a classless society is defined as one in which men would exercise a much greater, and equal, control over their individual destinies; would be liberated from the tyranny of their own creations such as the state and bureaucracy, capital and technology; would be productive rather than acquisitive; would find pleasure and support in their social co-operation with other men rather than antagonism and bitterness in the competition with them. Marx did not always express himself with the same optimism about the possibility of attaining this condition of society,[6] but he never ceased to regard it as the ideal. His notion of what would constitute self-determination for the individual was expressed in a variety of ways. In the first place, the individual had to be freed from determination by his class or occupation; as Marx wrote in *The German Ideology*, "... the communal relationship into which the individuals of a class entered, and which was determined by their common interests over against a third party was always a community to which these individuals belonged only as average individuals, only in so far as they lived within the conditions of existence of their class. It was a relationship in which they participated not as individuals but as members of a class. But with the community of revolutionary proletarians, who establish their control over the conditions of existence of themselves and the other members of society, it is just the reverse; the individuals participate as individuals. It is just this combination of individuals (assuming, of course, the advanced level of modern productive forces) which brings the conditions for the free development and activity of individuals under their own control; conditions which were formerly abandoned to chance and which had acquired an independent existence over against the separate individuals." Secondly, the individual had to be freed from domination by a remote, inaccessible and unaccountable government and administration, and to participate as fully as possible in deciding issues of general social importance. Marx held up as a practical instance of such participation the Paris Commune, in which the functions of government were undertaken by municipal councillors, chosen by universal suffrage, responsible and revocable at short term, and in which all public functions from those of the members of the Commune downwards were done *at workmen's* wages.

The sociological element in Marx's conception is to be found in his assertion that the principle of inequality is embodied in the institutions of social class—the division between owners of the means of production and non-owners—and more fundamentally in the division of labour in society, especially the division between manual and intellectual work. It follows that equality is to be attained by the abolition of classes, which will entail the suppression of the division of labour. Marx always insisted strongly upon this last condition. In *The German Ideology* he expressed it in a somewhat romantic form: ". . . as soon as the division of labour begins, each man has a particular, exclusive sphere of activity, which is forced upon him and from which he cannot escape. He is a hunter, a fisherman, a shepherd, or a critical critic,[7] and must remain so if he does not want to lose his means of livelihood; whereas in communist society, where nobody has one exclusive sphere of activity but each can become accomplished in any branch he wishes, production as a whole is regulated by society, thus making it possible for me to do one thing today and another tomorrow, to hunt in the morning, fish in the afternoon, rear cattle in the evening, criticize after dinner, in accordance with my inclination, without ever becoming hunter, fisherman, shepherd or critic"; but later, in the first volume of *Capital*, he conveyed the same idea in more realistic terms: ". . . the detail-worker of today, the limited individual, the mere bearer of a particular social function, will be replaced by the fully developed individual, for whom the different social functions he performs are but so many alternative modes of activity. One step already spontaneously taken towards effecting this revolution is the establishment of technical and agricultural schools, and of *écoles d'enseignement professionel*, in which the children of the working men receive some instruction in technology and in the practical handling of the various implements of labour. . . . there can be no doubt that when the working class comes into power . . . technical instruction, both theoretical and practical, will take its proper place in the working class schools." Marx's argument, therefore, is directed just as much against the idea of functional elites—even elites recruited solely on the basis of merit—as against the idea of classes. The division of labour, and above all the division between those who think and plan and those who merely perform the necessary manual labour, continually recreates the class system; and it confines the individual within a sphere of life which he has not chosen for himself and in which he cannot acquire the means to develop all his faculties.

The historical element in this conception has two aspects. First, Marx presents a historical scheme, applicable mainly within the area of Western civilization, in which the forms of domination and servitude—master and slave, feudal lord and serf, industrial capitalist and worker—constitute a series which is distinguished by an increasing awareness of the contrast between man's qualities as an individual and his qualities as a member of a social category. ". . . in the course of historical development . . . there emerges a distinction between the personal life of the individual and his life as it is determined by some branch of labour and the conditions pertaining to it . . . In a system of estates (and still more in the tribe) this is still concealed: for instance, a nobleman is always a nobleman, a commoner always a commoner, irrespective of his other relationships, a quality inseparable from his individuality. The distinction between the personal and the class individual, the accidental nature of conditions of life for the individual, appears only with the emergence of class, which itself is a product of the bourgeoisie. . . . The contradiction between the personality of the individual proletarian and the condition of life imposed on him, his labour, becomes evident to himself, for he is sacrificed from his youth onwards and has no opportunity of achieving within his own class the conditions which would place him in another class" (*The German Ideology*). To this series Marx added a further term, the classless society of the future in which there would no longer be any sharp contrast between the personal qualities of the individual and the conditions of his social life, in which each individual would be able to develop his faculties to the fullest extent and would experience limitation only as a natural being, who is obliged to produce his material means of existence and who is mortal.

Secondly, Marx regards the classless society as a form of society which is only conceivable, and can only be achieved, at the historical moment when capitalism attains its fullest development, because the consummation of capitalism produces for the first time a subject class—the proletariat—which contains within itself no elements of further social differentiation. When the proletariat has been liberated by the expropriation of the capitalist owners of industry it will create new social institutions which will express its own homogeneity and solidarity and preclude the formation of new privileged groups in society.

Few modern advocates of equality would dissent from Marx's moral ideal of the classless society; but they would question some of the sociological and historical arguments with which Marx explained the manner of its advent and defined its characteristics. They would object still more to what used to be the orthodox Marxist interpretation (but it has been changing in recent years) of the classless society, which reduced the concept to little more than a technical expression describing a state of affairs in which there is no private ownership of industry. The major objection to Marx's own account must be that it portrays the attainment of a classless society—of genuine equality and liberty—as a once-for-all affair: at one moment men are living in the egoistic, acquisitive, conflict-ridden world of capitalism; at the next, pre-history has come to an end and men are engaged in creating the new institutions of a classless society. This is not quite fair to Marx inasmuch as he allows for a period of transition between capitalism and socialism—described by that phrase of ill-omen "the dictatorship of the proletariat" —and for stages of development towards the "higher phase of communist society" (*Critique of the Gotha Programme*). But it is fair in the sense that Marx never for a moment considers the possibility that under certain circumstances new social distinctions and a new ruling class might emerge in the society which succeeds capitalism; for example, from the dictatorship of the proletariat itself, which is so easily transformed into the tyranny of a party. This is a point of weakness in the Marxist doctrine which the elite theorists, and notably Michels,[8] attacked so successfully; and a new cogency has been given to their criticisms by the experiences of the USSR and the East European countries under Stalin's rule. Thus, Raymond Aron is able to describe the classless society in these terms: "There is still, however, in such a society, a small number of men who in practice run the industrial undertakings, command the army, decide what proportion of the national resources should be allocated to saving and investment and fix scales of remuneration. This minority has infinitely more power than the political rulers in a democratic society, because both political and economic power are concentrated in their hands ... Politicians, trade union leaders, public officials, generals and managers all belong to one party and are part of an authoritarian organization. The unified elite has absolute and unbounded power. All intermediate bodies, all individual groupings, and particularly professional groups, are in fact controlled by delegates of the elite, or, if you prefer it, representatives of the State. ... A classless society leaves the mass of the population without any possible means of defence against the elite."[9]

Aron then considers an objection to this account, namely that the idea of a classless society is being confused with a more or less accurate picture of Soviet society, and he admits that "a different type of classless society is in theory possible. In present conditions, however, other types of classless society are extremely unlikely. In order to avoid a monopoly of power in the hands of the group of men in control of the state, it would be necessary to restore a large number of centres of power, the various undertakings or trusts should become the property of those working in them, of local or trade union communities, instead of the centralized state. At the present time such decentralization is unlikely to come about, for psychological and technical reasons ... It is possible to conceive also that the elite in power might not constitute a sort of religious and military sect and might be organized as a democratic party. There again, however, the idea which is possible in theory is extremely unlikely in practice ... Even more, the ideological monopoly preserved by the elite in power seems to me to correspond to an inherent requirement in such a regime ... In short, the unification of the elite is inseparable from the concentration of all economic and political power in its hands and that concentration is itself inseparable from the planning of an entirely collectivized economy."[10]

Is it possible to meet these objections and to formulate in a more acceptable way the ideal of an egalitarian society? Let us note, first, some important resemblances between the classless society in the USSR as described by Aron, and the mass society which C. Wright Mills portrays as developing in the USA. In a mass society, which Mills contrasts with a democratic "society of publics": "(1) far fewer people express opinions than receive them; for the community of publics becomes an abstract collection of individuals who receive impressions from the mass media. (2) The communications that prevail are so organized that it is difficult or impossible for the individual to answer back immediately or with any effect. (3) The realization of opinion in action is controlled by authorities who organize and control the channels of such action. (4) The mass has no autonomy from institutions; on the contrary, agents of authorized institutions penetrate this mass, reducing any autonomy it may have in the formation of opinion by discussion."[11] Among the most important structural characteristics of both the classless society and the mass society are the decline or disappearance of intermediate organizations—voluntary associations small enough for the individual to have an effective say in their activities—and the increasing distance between the leaders and the masses in all types of organization. It is obvious that these characteristics are very much more pronounced in the Soviet-type

societies than in the Western countries, where there is no
political or legal bar to the formation of associations, and
where open as well as hidden competition for the allegiance
of the citizens takes place between the large organizations;
but there are also common features which have been produced
by more general causes, among them the growth in the size
of organizations brought about by technological advances
(in production, communication, etc.), the increasing influence
and control exercised by the state over economic production,
irrespective of the type of economy, which is determined
very largely by the massive production of war materials, and
the international rivalry between nations organized on a
semi-war footing, which is favourable to the growth of
centralized and authoritarian political leadership.

Not all of these adverse influences can be combated
effectively within the limits of a single society; they also
call for changes in the relations between nations. Those
problems which can be dealt with on a national level arise
very largely from the size and complexity of organizations
and, as Aron points out, from the authoritarian tendencies
implicit in centralized economic planning, especially in a
collectivized economy. The attempt to solve them has to
proceed along several different lines, some of which have been
indicated in the previous chapter—the greatest possible
decentralization of political authority by the transfer of
responsibility for decisions, wherever feasible, to local and
regional councils and to voluntary associations, and the
extension of self-government to the economic field by the
creation of appropriate new institutions, such as the workers'
councils in present-day Yugoslavia. The danger that a new
ruling class of political bosses and industrial managers will
be formed in a collectivized economy can be met, not only
by the introduction of self-government in the factory, but

also by limiting the scope of collective ownership. It does not seem to me necessary to the attainment of an egalitarian society that all small-scale retail trading or farming, or semi-artisan production, should be absorbed into large collective enterprises. At the least, this should be treated as a practical question, and the propensity of such private economic activities to engender new social classes and new inequalities should be carefully studied in the light of experience. Similarly, the dangers of an intellectual dictatorship can be met by giving a large degree of autonomy to educational and cultural organizations.

In the intellectual sphere it is particularly important that there should be independent associations which compete with each other; not only in the case of sound and television broadcasting and the press, but also in book publishing and in scientific research. But this requirement is quite compatible with public ownership. The associations could well be owned or effectively controlled by their members, while being supported to a large extent by public funds and subject to general regulation by a national authority. This is already the situation of universities in most Western countries. The same principle can be applied also to the operation of industry and commerce. The individual enterprises may be owned, and most of their policies decided upon by those who work in them, and they may compete with each other in respect of price and quality at least as effectively as privately owned enterprises now do, while being subject to controls of various kinds in the interests of a national economic plan. The achievements of a system of this kind, which combines public ownership with a form of market economy, in Yugoslavia, show that although there are many practical difficulties this is a viable form of economic organization and no longer simply a Utopian dream.[12] There does not seem to be any reason for supposing that in advanced industrial societies, which do not have to engage in the arduous business of primary capital accumulation, the control of the economy as a whole by a central planning authority need be any more rigorous or authoritarian under a system of public owner-ship such as that which I have outlined than under a private enterprise system; for in both cases there will be very similar problems to be faced and similar techniques can be employed. In France, for example, the postwar economic planners have had very considerable powers and they have not been subject to any close control by the elected representatives of the people. In Britain the recently established National Economic Development Council, if its activities are to have any meaning, will be obliged to propose restraints and incentives, to be enforced by the central government, which will bring about the desired kind and rate of economic growth.

These considerations are sufficient, I think, to cast serious doubt upon Aron's assertion that it would be impossible to achieve, in a collectivized economy, a genuine decentraliza-tion of power, or to escape intellectual and cultural uni-formity. It is true, of course, that even in a classless society which had carried decentralization very far, and in which numerous independent associations flourished, there would exist some fundamental agreement among the members of society upon the general features of its organization. But this must be the case in any society which is to endure, and as we have seen, those who regard democracy as being sustained by a plurality of competing elites still introduce the qualification that the competition must not be pushed to extremes and that there must be an underlying consensus of opinion. The hope of those who advocate equality is that the experience of living in a society which was drawing rapidly closer to this ideal would eventually persuade men of its value. If this occurred, there would remain all manner of intellectual disagreements and of choices as to a personal way of life, but there would be general agreement upon the desirability of social equality and opposition to those inequalities which produce and maintain lasting distinctions between whole categories of men.

Let me now return to another problem which is posed by Marx's conception of a classless society. According to Marx, the division of labour is not only in itself an impediment to the full development of each individual, a form of bondage, but is also the source from which arise the major social classes, which establish still more obdurate limitations of human freedom. The division of labour has, therefore, to be "overcome": that is, abolished and transcended. But does it make sense to speak of "abolishing" the division of labour in a modern industrial society? At first sight the problem seems more intractable now than in Marx's own day, for the specialization of occupations, including intellectual occupations, has proceeded rapidly, and in the sphere of industrial mass-production the subdivision of tasks has reached a point where the individual worker appears more and more as an adjunct to the machine, whose daily work is confined to the performance of a few simple, thoughtless and repetitive movements. Nevertheless, there have been other changes in work, and a new range of possibilities can now be seen, which make Marx's vision of the future a great deal more plausible. First, there have been changes in the nature of occupations, brought about especially by the development of automation. The effect of automation is to eliminate the worker on the assembly line and to replace him by a more educated and responsible individual whose function is to supervise very complicated chains of production which are controlled in detail by machines. At present these changes affect only a small part of industry, but they will become increasingly important. Secondly, the high productivity of modern industry has already made possible a reduction of working hours, and its accelerating rate of growth will bring within the capacity of all the advanced industrial countries, in the next decade or two, the establishment of a working week of some twenty-five or thirty hours. These countries are about to produce a new and revolutionary phenomenon; namely, a "leisure class" which comprises the whole population. In the USA the first signs of such a condition of society can already be seen; in 1962, for example, the New York branch of the International Brotherhood of Electrical Workers gained for its members a basic five hour day and twenty-five hour week.[13] Thirdly, if there were introduced in publicly owned industries the kind of self-management which I discussed earlier, and if this type of public ownership were established in all large enterprises, the range of the work activities of manual and clerical workers would be considerably extended. The individual worker would no longer be confined within his specialized task, but would also take part in the planning and management of production.

Together, these various changes in the organization of working life would modify profoundly the sense of the division of labour. The individual with abundant leisure would have the opportunity, as Marx believed, to devote himself to more than one activity, to express himself in diverse fields of endeavour, both physical and intellectual; and even as an economic producer he would find more occasion to develop all-round abilities by participating in the work of management and by learning something of the science and technology upon which the operations of industry are based. The division of labour would become more evidently a technique which men have to use in producing their means of life, but which they must also control; it would no longer shape and constrict the whole of their lives, turning one man irrevocably into a worker on the assembly line, another into a clerk, and a third into a tycoon. Such changes imply, and they are already beginning to produce, a vast expansion of education in all its forms—an extension of the period of universal secondary education, higher education for a large proportion of those between the ages of eighteen and twenty-one, adult education on a large scale, with special facilities for those who decide at a mature age to prepare themselves for a new occupation—and the provision, on an immense scale, of equipment for sport and recreation. Perhaps I may conclude this discussion, and at the same time illustrate how slowly new and radical ideas make their way in the world, by quoting from one of the most eminent of British economists, whose vision of the role of labour in a future society was very close to that of Marx. Alfred Marshall, in an essay on "The Future of the Working Classes" which was published in 1873 wrote: "That men do habitually sustain hard corporeal work for eight, ten or twelve hours a day, is a fact so familiar to us that we scarcely realize the extent to which it governs the moral and mental history of the world; we scarcely realize how subtle, all-pervading and powerful may be the effect of the work of man's body in dwarfing the growth of the man . . . Work, in its best sense, the healthy energetic exercise of faculties, is the aim of life, is life itself; and in this sense every one [in the ideal society which Marshall conceives] would be a worker more completely than now. But men would have ceased to carry on mere physical work to such an extent as to dull their higher energies. In the bad sense, in which work crushes a man's life, it would be regarded as wrong. The active vigour of the people would continually increase; and in each successive generation it would be more completely true that every man was by occupation a gentleman. . . . that condition which we have pictured . . . a condition in which every man's energies and abilities will be fully developed—a condition in which men will work not less than they do now but more; only, to use a good old phrase, most of their work will be a work of love; it will be a work which, whether conducted for payment or not, will exercise and nurture their faculties. Manual work, carried to such an excess that it leaves little opportunity for the free growth of his higher nature, that alone will be absent; but that *will* be absent. In so far as the working classes are men who have such excessive work to do, in so far will the working classes have been abolished."[14]

So far I have considered mainly those objections to the idea of a classless, egalitarian society which take as their main theme the dangers of intellectual tyranny and political dictatorship. There is, however, another important line of criticism which brings to light a different aspect of the problem of elites. It has often been maintained, in one form or another, that the advancement of civilization has depended, and does always depend, upon the activities of small minorities of exceptionally gifted people. Ortega y Gasset says it in *The Revolt of the Masses*: "As one advances in life, one realizes more and more that the majority of men—and of women—are incapable of any other effort than that strictly imposed on them as a reaction to external compulsion. And for that reason, the few individuals we have come across who are capable of a spontaneous and joyous effort stand out isolated, monumentalized, so to speak, in our experience. These are the select men, the nobles, the only ones who are active and not merely reactive, for whom life is a perpetual striving, an incessant course of training."[15] In a similar manner, Clive Bell, in his book *Civilization*, argues that a civilized society is characterized by reasonableness and a sense of values, and that these qualities can only be produced, implanted and sustained by an elite. Now some part of what is asserted by these writers is undoubtedly true; namely, that civilization has been greatly advanced by the work of exceptional men. (It has also been greatly retarded by the activities of other exceptional men.) But this is not to say that such men, with their associates or followers, form a social elite, still less that they are in the majority of cases a *ruling* elite. They may have little social prestige, or be treated with active disdain by the rulers of society; they may be dependent financially upon the patronage of an upper class, without forming part of it. Their contribution to society is of an individual kind, not ordinarily dependent upon the formation of a distinctive social group; very often it is more strongly affected by the support and enthusiasm which their work calls forth in a whole population (as in fifth-century Athens) or in a whole class (as in Renaissance Italy or in eighteenth-century France). Exceptional men might perhaps be regarded as forming an elite in the first of the senses which Pareto gave to the term—namely, the category of those who have the highest ability in their branch of activity—except that in this sense many activities which have little or nothing to do with the advance of civilization would be included, and that the elites so defined would be made up of talented individuals rather than of those who have exceptional creative powers. It would really be better to use some other term; for example, the term "creative minority," which Arnold Toynbee seemed to be using in his *Study of History* to refer, not to an elite group, but to a simple plurality of individuals. Thus he says that "In all acts of social creation the creators are either creative individuals or, at most, creative minorities . . . "[16]

Those who seek to defend the elite doctrines by referring to the importance of intellectual and artistic creativity commit two errors: first, they neglect the vital interplay between creative individuals and the society in which they live—which is perhaps most evident in the case of scientific work, but is also to be traced in the history of painting or architecture, in literature, in religious movements and in moral reforms—and secondly, they assume that such individuals associate together as an elite or elites which can only exist in a hierarchically ordered society, and which can exist best in a society divided into stable and enduring classes. In this last conception, as it is expressed, for example, by T. S. Eliot in his *Notes Towards the Definition of Culture*, the subject of discussion is apt to change from the creation of culture to the transmission of culture. In Eliot's view there are, in every complex society, a number of levels of culture; it is important for the health of society that these different levels should be related to each other, but also that they should remain distinct, and that the manners and taste of society as a whole should be influenced by the highest culture. This can only happen, since culture is transmitted primarily through the family, if there exists an upper class composed of families which are able to maintain over several generations a settled way of life. Eliot admits that the existence of an upper class does not guarantee a high culture: " . . . the 'conditions of culture' which I set forth do not necessarily produce the higher civilization: I assert only that when they are absent, the higher civilization is unlikely to be found."[17] Nevertheless, it *may* be found. We have as yet no direct experience of the way of life of an egalitarian society, and we can do no more than estimate the probability of its being able to create and preserve a high level of culture. Creation is an individual act, but it is facilitated by a general enthusiasm and liveliness in society at large, and we may reasonably expect that an egalitarian society, in which leisure was widespread and individuals were encouraged to develop their talents, would be at least as creative as those which accomplished great things in earlier periods when the economic conditions and the class structure of society were being rapidly transformed. As to the conservation and transmission of a high culture, we may well dissent from the view that it has been, and must be, primarily the work of the family. In the past, many other social groups—religious associations, philosophical schools, academies—have been at least as important as the family in transmitting culture; the family, i.e. the families of the upper class in society, have usually passed on, if they have passed on at all, something that has been conserved and kept alive elsewhere, by associations which enjoyed no great stability of membership from generation to generation. In a classless society the distance between high culture and lower types of culture would be less great, and regional and local diversity might become more pronounced; and the cultural heritage would be handed on, even more than in the past, by educational institutions and voluntary associations of every kind, and less than formerly by particular families. It is possible, too, that the conservation of culture, which is bound up inextricably in present-day societies with the maintenance of class privileges, would be less strongly emphasized—or at least change its aspect—and come to be taken much more for granted; while the power to create new forms of culture, to make new discoveries in the arts and sciences, would be more highly regarded and encouraged.

The theorists of elites defend, by these various means, the legacy from the inegalitarian societies of the past, while making concessions to the spirit of equality. They insist strongly upon an absolute distinction between rulers and ruled, which they present as a scientific law, but they reconcile democracy with this state of affairs by defining it as competition between elites. They accept and justify the division of society into classes, but endeavour to make this division more palatable by describing the upper classes as elites, and by suggesting that the elites are composed of the most able individuals, regardless of their social origins. Their case depends, to a large extent, upon substituting for the idea of equality the idea of equality of opportunity. But this latter notion, besides having quite a different moral significance, is actually self-contradictory. Equality of opportunity, as the expression is habitually used, pre-supposes inequality, since "opportunity" means "the opportunity to rise to a higher level in a stratified society." At the same time, it pre-supposes equality, for it implies that the inequalities embedded in this stratified society have to be counteracted in every generation so that individuals can really develop their personal abilities; and every investigation of the conditions for equality of opportunity, for example in the sphere of education, has shown how strong and pervasive is the influence upon individual life-chances of the entrenched distinctions of social class. Equality of opportunity would only become a reality in a society without classes or elites, and the notion itself would then be otiose, for the equal life-chances of individuals in each new generation would be matters of fact, and the idea of opportunity would signify, not the struggle to rise into a higher social class, but the possibility for each individual to develop fully those qualities of intellect and sensibility which he has as a person, in an unconstrained association with other men.

# NOTES

[1] J. J. Rousseau, *A Dissertation on the Origin and Foundation of the Inequality of Mankind* (Everyman edition), p. 160.

[2] It is admirably expounded in R. H. Tawney's *Equality*.

[3] Surprisingly, this is often held against him, instead of being regarded as a mark of wisdom, and of profound faith in the creative capacities of men which were manifest even within the constraints of class societies and would be so much more easily made effective when those constraints were removed.

[4] See T. B. Bottomore (ed.), *Karl Marx: Early Writings*.

[5] See, for example, his discussion in *Capital*, Vol. I, of the means to overcome the harmful effects of the division of labour, and in *Capital*, Vol. III, of the conditions of human freedom; his praise of the Paris Commune for its institution of genuinely democratic self-government, in *The Civil War in France*; and his comments upon the programme of the Socialist Workers' Party of Germany in *Critique of the Gotha Programme*.

6 For instance, in the passage on human freedom in *Capital*, Vol. III, Marx declares that the sphere of economic production is a realm of necessity "under any possible mode of production." "The realm of freedom only begins, in fact, where that labour which is determined by need and external purpose, ceases; it is therefore, by its very nature, outside the sphere of material production proper."

7 Marx refers here to the Young Hegelians who called their modified Hegelian philosophy "critical criticism."

8 See especially, *Political Parties*, Part VI, Chap. 2.

9 Art. cit., *British Journal of Sociology*, I (2), p. 131.

10 Ibid., pp. 131-2.

11 C. Wright Mills, *The Power Elite*, p. 304.

12 For a brief account of the Yugoslav system, see Fred Singleton and Tony Topham, "Yugoslav Workers' Control: The Latest Phase", *New Left Review* (18), pp. 73-84.

13 The division of labour and the growth of leisure are examined at length from a point of view which is very similar to my own in Georges Friedmann, *The Anatomy of Work*.

14 Alfred Marshall, "The Future of the Working Classes" in A. C. Pigou (ed.), *Memorials of Alfred Marshall*, pp. 101-18.

15 op. cit., p. 49.

16 *A Study of History*, Vol. III, p. 239. However, in his concluding volume, in which he reconsiders his work, Toynbee approaches more closely the elite theories, in saying: "By a creative minority I mean a ruling minority in which the creative faculty in human nature finds opportunities for expressing itself in effective action for the benefit of all participants in the society . . . By a dominant minority I mean a ruling minority that rules less by attraction and more by force" (op. cit., Vol. XII, *Reconsiderations*, p. 305).

17 op. cit., p. 49.

# SELECTED BIBLIOGRAPHY

*General Studies of Elites*

ARON, RAYMOND, "Social Structure and the Ruling Class", *British Journal of Sociology*, I (1), March, 1950, pp. 1–16 and I (2), June, 1950, pp. 126–43.

ARON, RAYMOND, "Classe sociale, classe politique, classe dirigeante", *European Journal of Sociology*, I (2), 1960, pp. 260–81.

BORKENAU, FRANZ, *Pareto* (London, Chapman & Hall, 1936).

BURNHAM, JAMES, *The Machiavellians: Defenders of Freedom* (London, Putnam & Co., 1943).

CLIFFORD-VAUGHAN, MICHALINA, "Some French Concepts of Elites", *British Journal of Sociology*, XI (4), December, 1960, pp. 319–31.

COLE, G. D. H., *Studies in Class Structure* (London, Routledge & Kegan Paul, 1955), Chap. V, "Elites in British Society".

DREITZEL, HANS P., *Elitebegriff und Sozialstruktur* (Stuttgart, Ferdinand Enke, 1962).

GINSBERG, M., "The Sociology of Pareto", in *Reason and Unreason in Society* (London, Longmans, Green & Co., 1947).

JAEGGI, URS, *Die gesellschaftliche Elite: Eine Studie zum Problem der sozialen Macht* (Bern, Paul Haupt, 1960).

LASSWELL, HAROLD D., LERNER, DANIEL, and ROTHWELL, C. EASTON, *The Comparative Study of Elites* (Hoover Institute Studies, Series B: Elites, No. 1, Stanford, 1952).

MEISEL, JAMES H., *The Myth of the Ruling Class: Gaetano Mosca and the Elite* (Ann Arbor, University of Michigan Press, 1958) [Contains a bibliography of Mosca's writings].

MILLS, C. WRIGHT, *The Power Elite* (New York, Oxford University Press, 1956).

MOSCA, GAETANO, *The Ruling Class* (New York, McGraw-Hill, 1939).

NADEL, S. F., "The Concept of Social Elites", *International Social Science Bulletin*, VIII (3), 1956, pp. 413-24.

OSSOWSKI, STANISLAW, *Class Structure in the Social Consciousness* (London, Routledge & Kegan Paul, 1963).

PARETO, VILFREDO, *Les systèmes socialistes* (Paris, Marcel Giard, 1902).

PARETO, VILFREDO, *The Mind and Society* (4 vols. London, Jonathan Cape, 1935) [English translation of *Trattato di Sociologia Generale*, 1915-19].

SCHUMPETER, J. A., *Imperialism and Social Classes* (Oxford, Basil Blackwell, 1951).

SERENO, RENZO, "The Anti-Aristotelianism of Gaetano Mosca and its Fate", *Ethics*, XLVIII (4), July, 1938.

### Political Elites

GUTTSMAN, W. L., *The British Political Elite* (London, MacGibbon & Kee, 1963).

McKENZIE, R. T., *British Political Parties* (London, Heinemann, 2nd edn. 1963).

MARVICK, DWAINE (ed.), *Political Decision-Makers* (Glencoe, The Free Press, 1961) [The Introduction provides a survey of current research].

MATTHEWS, D. R., *The Social Background of Political Decision-Makers* (New York, Doubleday, 1954).

MICHELS, ROBERT, *Political Parties* (Glencoe, The Free Press, 1949) [English trans. of *Zür Soziologie des Parteiwesens in der modernen Demokratie*, 2nd edn., Leipzig, 1925].

OSTROGORSKI, M., *Democracy and the Organization of Political Parties* (2 vols. London, Macmillan, 1908) [English trans. of *La démocratie et l'organisation des partis politiques*, Paris, 1903].

RUNCIMAN, W. G., *Social Science and Political Theory* (Cambridge, Cambridge University Press, 1963) Chap. IV "Elites and Oligarchies".

### Owners and Managers of Industry

ACTON SOCIETY TRUST, *Management Succession* (London, Acton Society Trust, 1956).

BALTZELL, E. DIGBY, *An American Business Aristocracy* (New York, Collier Books, 1962; originally published as *Philadelphia Gentlemen: The Making of a National Upper Class*, 1958).

BERLE, A. A. and MEANS, G. C., *The Modern Corporation and Private Property* (New York, Macmillan, 1933).

BURNHAM, JAMES, *The Managerial Revolution* (London, Putnam & Co., 1943).

CLEMENTS, R. V., *Managers: A Study of their Careers in Industry* (London, Allen & Unwin, 1958).

COPEMAN, G. H., *Leaders of British Industry: A Study of the Careers of more than a Thousand Public Company Directors* (London, Gee & Co., 1955).

FLORENCE, P. SARGANT, *The Logic of British and American Industry* (London, Routledge & Kegan Paul, 1953).

MILLER, WILLIAM (ed.), *Men in Business: Essays on the Historical Role of the Entrepreneur* (New York, Harper & Row, new edn. 1962).

TAUSSIG, F. W. and JOSLYN, C. S., *American Business Leaders* (New York, The Macmillan Co., 1932).

VEBLEN, THORSTEIN, *The Engineers and the Price System* (New York, The Viking Press, 1921).

WARNER, LLOYD W. and ABEGGLEN, JAMES C., *Big Business Leaders in America* (New York, Harper, 1955).

### Bureaucrats

ARMSTRONG, JOHN A., *The Soviet Bureaucratic Elite: A Case Study of the Ukrainian Apparatus* (London, Stevens & Sons, 1959).

BENDIX, R., *Higher Civil Servants in American Society* (Boulder, University of Colorado Press, 1949).

BLAU, PETER M., *Bureaucracy in Modern Society* (New York, Random House, 1956).

BOTTOMORE, T. B., "Higher Civil Servants in France", *Transactions of the Second World Congress of Sociology* (London, International Sociological Association, 1954), Vol. II, pp. 143–52.

DJILAS, M., *The New Class* (London, Thames & Hudson, 1957).

EISENSTADT, S. N., *The Political Systems of Empires: The Rise and Fall of the Historical Bureaucratic Empires* (New York, Collier-Macmillan, 1963).

KELSALL, R. K., *Higher Civil Servants in Britain* (London, Routledge & Kegan Paul, 1955).

KINGSLEY, J. DONALD, *Representative Bureaucracy* (Yellow Springs, Antioch Press, 1944).

STEWARD, JULIAN H., *Irrigation Civilizations: A Comparative Study* (Washington, Pan American Union, 1955).

WEBER, MAX, "Bureaucracy" in *From Max Weber* ed. by H. H. Gerth and C. Wright Mills (London, Kegan Paul, 1947).

WITTFOGEL, K. A., *Oriental Despotism* (New Haven, Yale University Press, 1957).

### Intellectuals

ARON, RAYMOND, *The Opium of the Intellectuals* (London, Secker & Warburg, 1957).

BENDA, JULIEN, *La trahison des clercs* (Paris, Grasset, 1927).

BODIN, LOUIS, *Les intellectuels* (Paris, Presses Universitaires de France, 1962).

DE HUSZAR, GEORGE B., *The Intellectuals: A Controversial Portrait* (Glencoe, The Free Press, 1960).

GRAMSCI, ANTONIO, *Gli Intellettuali e l'organizzazione della cultura* (Milan, Einaudi, 1955).

LE GOFF, JACQUES, *Les intellectuels au Moyen Age* (Paris, Editions du Seuil, 1957).

LIPSET, S. M., *Political Man* (London, Heinemann, 1960), Chap. X, "American Intellectuals: Their Politics and Status".

MANNHEIM, KARL, *Ideology and Utopia* (London, Kegan Paul, 1936) Chap. III, sect. 4, "The sociological problem of the 'intelligentsia' ".

MANNHEIM, KARL, *Man and Society in an Age of Reconstruction* (London, Kegan Paul, 1940) Part II, Chaps. VIII–IX.

MICHELS, ROBERT, "Intellectuals", *Encyclopaedia of the Social Sciences*, ed. by E. R. A. Seligman (New York, Macmillan, 1932) Vol. VIII, pp. 118–26 [An extensive bibliography is appended to the article].

WEBER, MAX, "The Chinese Literati" in *From Max Weber* ed. by H. H. Gerth and C. Wright Mills (London, Kegan Paul, 1947).

### The Circulation of Elites

BRINTON, CRANE, *The Anatomy of Revolution* (New York, rev. edn., 1957).

DAHRENDORF, RALF, "Über einige Probleme der soziologischen Theorie der Revolution", *European Journal of Sociology*, II (1), 1961, pp. 153–62.

GIRARD, ALAIN, *La réussite sociale en France: ses caractéres, ses lois, s es effets* (Paris, Presses Universitaires de France, 1961).

KOLABINSKA, MARIE, *La circulation des élites en France: Etude historique depuis la fin du XIe siècle jusqu'à la Grande Révolution* (Lausanne, Imprimeries Réunies, 1912).

LIPSET, S. M. and BENDIX, R., *Social Mobility in Industrial Society* (Berkeley, University of California Press, 1949).

MARSH, ROBERT M., *The Mandarins: The Circulation of Elites in China, 1600–1900* (Glencoe, The Free Press, 1961).

MILLER, S. M., "Comparative Social Mobility", *Current Sociology* IX (1), 1960, 89 pp.

PIRENNE, HENRI, "Les périodes de l'histoire sociale du capitalisme", *Bulletin de l'Académie royale de Belgique*, mai, 1914 [English trans. in the *American Historical Review*, April, 1914].


### Elites in the Underdeveloped Countries

ALMOND, G. A. and COLEMAN, J. S., *The Politics of the Developing Areas* (Princeton, Princeton University Press, 1960) [Contains five useful area studies on South-east Asia, South Asia, Sub-Saharan Africa, the Near East and Latin America].

BERGER, MORROE, *Bureaucracy and Society in Modern Egypt: A Study of the Higher Civil Service* (Princeton, Princeton University Press, 1957).

FRIEDMANN, GEORGES, *Problèmes d'Amérique latine* (Paris, Gallimard, 1959).

FRIEDMANN, GEORGES, *Signal d'une troisième voie?* (Paris, Gallimard, 1961).

HODGKIN, THOMAS, *African Political Parties: An Introductory Guide* (Harmondsworth, Penguin Books, 1961).

KERR, CLARK, DUNLOP, JOHN T., HARBISON, FREDERICK H. and MYERS, CHARLES A., *Industrialism and Industrial Man* (Cambridge,

Harvard University Press, 1960) [See especially Chap. 3, "The Industrializing Elites and their Strategies"].

LIEUWEN, EDWIN, *Arms and Politics in Latin America* (New York, Frederick A. Praeger, rev. edn. 1961).

MISRA, B. B., *The Indian Middle Classes* (London, Oxford University Press, 1961).

NIEL, R. VAN, *The Emergence of the Modern Indonesian Elite* (The Hague, W. Van Hoewe, 1960).

PYE, LUCIAN W., "Armies in the Process of Political Modernization", *European Journal of Sociology*, II (1), 1961, pp. 82–92.

SHILS, E., *The Intellectual Between Tradition and Modernity: The Indian Situation* (The Hague, Mouton & Co., 1961; *Comparative Studies in Society and History*, Supplement I).

SMYTHE, H. H. and SMYTHE, M. M., *The New Nigerian Elite* (Stanford, Stanford University Press, 1960).

UNESCO, *International Social Science Bulletin*, VIII (3), 1956. Symposium on "African Elites", pp. 413–88.

WERTHEIM, W. F., *Indonesian Society in Transition: A Study of Social Change* (The Hague and Bandung, W. Van Hoeve, 2nd edn. 1959).

### Elites and Democracy

BELL, CLIVE, *Civilization: An Essay* (London, Chatto & Windus, 1928).

MANNHEIM, KARL, *Man and Society in an Age of Reconstruction* (London, Kegan Paul, 1940), Part II, Chaps. II–VII.

MANNHEIM, KARL, *Essays on the Sociology of Culture* (London, Routledge & Kegan Paul, 1956), Part III "The Democratization of Culture".

SCHUMPETER, J. A., *Capitalism, Socialism and Democracy* (London, Allen & Unwin, 1943).

UNESCO, *Democracy in a World of Tensions*, ed. by Richard McKeon (Paris, UNESCO, 1951) [See especially the essays contributed by G. C. Field, Lord Lindsay, S. Ossowski and Ithiel de Sola Pool].

### Other Works Cited in the Text

ARON, RAYMOND, *Paix et Guerre entre les nations* (Paris, Calmann-Lévy, 1962).

BLOCH, MARC, *Feudal Society* (London, Routledge & Kegan Paul, 1961).

BOTTOMORE, T. B. (ed.), *Karl Marx: Early Writings* (London, Watts & Co., 1963).

CROCE, BENEDETTO, *Historical Materialism and the Economics of Karl Marx* (London, Howard Latimer, 1913).

ELIOT, T. S., *Notes Towards the Definition of Culture* (London, Faber & Faber, 1948).

FINER, S.E., *The Man on Horseback: The Role of the Military in Politics* (London, Pall Mall Press, 1962).

FRIEDMANN, GEORGES, *The Anatomy of Work* (London, Heinemann, 1962).

FRIEDRICH, CARL J., *The New Image of the Common Man* (Boston, Beacon Press, 2nd edn., 1950).

GRAMSCI, ANTONIO, *Note sul Machiavelli, sulla politica e sullo stato moderno* (Milan, Einaudi, 1955).

LÜTHY, H., *The State of France* (London, Secker & Warburg, 1955).

NOMAD, MAX, *Rebels and Renegades* (New York, Macmillan, 1932).

ORTEGA Y GASSET, JOSÉ, *The Revolt of the Masses* (1930; English trans. 1932; new edn. London, Allen & Unwin, 1961).

PIGOU, A, C. (ed.), *Memorials of Alfred Marshall* (London, Macmillan, 1925).

ROUSSEAU, J. J., *A Dissertation on the Origin and Foundation of the Inequality of Mankind* (in the Everyman edition of *The Social Contract and Discourses*; London, Dent & Sons, 1913).

SAMPSON, ANTHONY, *Anatomy of Britain* (London, Hodder & Stoughton, 1962).

SIEGFRIED, ANDRÉ, *De la IIIème à la IVème République* (Paris, Grasset, 1957).

STRACHEY, JOHN, *Contemporary Capitalism* (London, Gollancz, 1956).

TAWNEY, R. H., *Equality* (London, Allen & Unwin, 4th edn. 1952).

TITMUSS, RICHARD M., *Income Distribution and Social Change* (London, Allen & Unwin, 1962).

TOYNBEE, A. J., *A Study of History* (12 vols. London, Oxford University Press, 1934–61).

WEBER, MAX, "Politics as a Vocation" in *From Max Weber* ed. by H. H. Gerth and C. Wright Mills (London, Kegan Paul, 1947).

WEBER, MAX, *The Methodology of the Social Sciences* (Glencoe, The Free Press, 1949).

WILLIAMS, RAYMOND, *Culture and Society* (Harmondsworth, Penguin Books, 1961).

# INDEX